ON THE BALL: DOUBLES TENNIS TACTICS FOR RECREATIONAL PLAYERS

ON TH

BY GYATA STORMON

EBALL

Doubles Tennis Tactics for Recreational Players

On the Ball: Doubles Tennis Tactics for Recreational Players

Copyright © 2019 by Gyata Stormon. All rights reserved.
ISBN: 978-1-797637-52-5 (paperback)

Court diagrams and Shot Cycle diagrams © 2019 Gyata Stormon.
Do not reproduce without permission: ontheballbook@gmail.com.

Published in the United States by Gyata Stormon, www.ontheballbook.com.
Printed by Amazon's Kindle Direct Publishing in the USA.
Ebook version also available from Amazon.

✉ Subscribe to the On the Ball e-newsletter: www.ontheballbook.com/subscribe

Cover and back cover photos by Thomas Kilgour, with thanks to the Wailea Tennis Club, Maui, HI.
Mixed-doubles partner on cover, Chuck Stormon.
Inside photos as credited.

Copyediting by Tina Grenis.
Tennis content editing by Valerie Clarke.

Cover and book design by Art Kilgour, WriteDesign: writedesign.ca

Dedicated to my mother and first practice partner:
MARLING KILGOUR 1923–2006

Ottawa Tennis Club, circa 1950

6

TABLE OF CONTENTS

Preface 9
Introduction 13

CHAPTER 1 ORIENTATION
1.1 The Shot Cycle 16
1.2 Court Geography 21

CHAPTER 2 STARTING THE POINT
2.1 The Four Starting Positions 30
2.2 Choosing a Receiving Side 32
2.3 The Server 35
2.4 Server's Partner 43
2.5 The Receiver 51
2.6 Receiver's Partner 61
2.7 Serving Team Plays 67

CHAPTER 3 ONE UP AND ONE BACK
3.1 One-Up and One-Back Formation 86
3.2 The Net Player 88
3.3 The Baseline Player 103
3.4 The Lob 114
3.5 Playing Straight 121

CHAPTER 4 IN THE ZONE
4.1 Playing in the Same Zone 130
4.2 The Approach Shot 138
4.3 The Workhorse 149
4.4 The Terminator 157
4.5 The Dogfight 163
4.6 Covering the Lob 166
4.7 Both Up Against Both Back 171
4.8 Both Back 173

CHAPTER 5 PRACTICE SKILLS
5.1 Why Practice? 184
5.2 Half-Court Drills 188
5.3 Full-Court Drills 194
5.4 In the Zone Drills 201
5.5 Serve and Return Drills 208
5.6 Games for Two or Three 215
5.7 Warm-ups 220

Conclusion 225
Appendix: Guide for Beginners 226
Bibliography 229
Glossary of Tennis Terms 230

8

PREFACE

On the Ball could vastly improve your doubles game. It might even change your life. Before we get started you probably want to know something about who I am and why I'm qualified to teach you about doubles tennis tactics.

Almost everything I know and teach about doubles has come from study, practice, competition and teaching. I began to play at age 10. Although I learned my strokes from a public parks instructor, I learned to play the game playing with my mom between lessons.

I loved competition and was a natural doubles player. As a fearless volleyer, I preferred the net over the baseline even in singles. This was the 1970s and I became one of the top 10 Canadian juniors.

I spent my adolescent summers competing in the Pacific Northwest and Eastern Canada. In college, I was a scholarship athlete at the University of Iowa, winning the Big Ten Doubles Championship in 1981. Yet, other than being encouraged to serve and volley on both first and second serves, I don't remember receiving specific doubles coaching in college. I learned and trained for singles.

Like many players who don't go on to play professionally, I left tennis after college. My body was tired and I wanted to do other things. I rediscovered tennis while living in a spiritual community in India from 1995 to 1999. There I was part of an active community that was exploring the relationship between tennis and meditation (Spang, 1998). In 1995, I became inspired to formally train as a tennis coach in the Canadian system. I learned a game-based approach, teaching students how to play the game (tactics) while simultaneously developing technique.

I played and competed a lot from 2006 to 2013. I won the Canadian Doubles Championship three times in the 45s age group, represented

Gyata Stormon with her brother Art in 1972.

Gyata Stormon (right) with partner Anne Marie Vick (center) and referee Melissa Jackson, 2011.

Canada in the Senior World Championships, and played at USTA Nationals three times at the 4.5 level. Truly the greatest gift of these years was my regular doubles partner, Anne Marie Vick. We studied and practiced all aspects of doubles and put them to the test during the rigors of competition playing USTA matches and competing at the Grass Court Senior Nationals.

In 2007, I began coaching teams at the NTRP* 3.0, 3.5 and 4.0 levels. I focused on teaching singles and doubles tactics, encouraging my students to make the most of the strokes they'd already developed. Players improved, they got bumped up, and most of my teams won their seasons.

Watching my students and their opponents, I noticed that most players were ineffective when both partners came into net. The lob was much more of a weapon than I remembered from junior tennis, and doubles teams were either confused about who was supposed to take the lob or both hung back around the service line to protect against it.

---

* The National Tennis Rating Program (NTRP) is a classification system developed by the United States Tennis Association (USTA) in 1978. It identifies and describes the general characteristics of 13 different levels of tennis-playing ability among adults for the purpose of providing comparable levels of ability for league competition. See: www.usta.com/tennis/ntrp.

This observation opened my mind to discovering new possibilities. First I read and practiced the theories and patterns described by Louis Cayer in his book *Doubles Tennis Tactics* (2004). Although it was helpful in many ways, this work was geared toward high-performance players. Next I began to study and practice the material from Helle Sparre Viragh's book, *Dynamite Doubles* (2004). Her doubles system includes a staggered, both-up-at-net system, where one player has the role to hit winning volleys and the other helps to set up her partner and cover the lobs. In 2011, I had the opportunity to train personally with Helle.

Shortly after I completed the first draft of this book, I attended a two-day camp with Gigi Fernandez, the 17-time Grand Slam Doubles Champion. She teaches adults at small group events and online through her extensive doubles.tv program. Although my approach to coaching doubles was already well established, I was able to clarify my thoughts and this book includes new insights that immediately made sense to me.

I've been writing and preparing notes for my students for many years, believing that it only makes sense to accelerate the learning process with off-court studying. Eventually, I had so many drafts of notes for different level students, and so many pages I still wanted to write, that it was time to put it all together in one convenient book.

Therefore, I want to acknowledge my students. I really do learn from them every time I step onto the court to teach. Their enthusiasm, encouragement and thirst for learning has helped bring *On the Ball* to life.

— *Gyata Stormon*

Gyata Stormon is a PTA Certified Level 1 Coach (Canada, 1995) and a PTR Certified Professional (Adult Development, 2018). She holds a M.A. in Sociology (1989), is a New York State Licensed Massage Therapist (2002), and a Certified Forrest Yoga Teacher (2013).

INTRODUCTION

On the Ball: Doubles Tennis Tactics for Recreational Players is a practical guide for recreational players of any level who want to improve and enjoy the game more.

It's ideal for doubles partners and playing groups seeking clearer understanding of how to work together to truly be On the Ball. All ages of players, including high school students, can benefit. Players who are "on the ball" are knowledgeable, competent and alert. This book illuminates all three of these qualities in relation to modern doubles tactics.

On the Ball provides up-to-date knowledge about doubles and presents it in an easily understood format with plenty of diagrams. You'll learn to be at the right place on the court, ready and on the balls of your feet as your opponent hits. As you hit, you'll have your eyes on the ball and the confidence of knowing exactly where to aim.

Next, as you study and practice the material, your competence on the court will improve. An extensive Practice Skills chapter provides you with relevant drills to help you integrate the material from the earlier chapters.

Finally, On the Ball addresses the quality of being alert, teaching you how to be present during each stroke that makes up a point, game, set and match.

If you're new to tennis doubles, On the Ball will get you playing smart doubles from the get go. You'll find some tips about how to get started in the Appendix.

If you're a seasoned doubles player, On the Ball will take you to a higher level through improved tactical awareness. You'll learn new movement patterns and places to hit the ball. I teach high percentage doubles tactics that will win you more points and matches in the long run.

If you're a left-handed player, On the Ball includes specific suggestions to help you discover and make the most of your advantage. Since right-handed players are in the majority, right-handedness is assumed in the text and diagrams unless otherwise stated.

If you're a tennis coach, On the Ball will provide you with many ways to enhance your doubles coaching. As a doubles' specialist coach, I've tested and used this information and know that the topics and diagrams can be easily developed into lesson plans.

I recommend reading the first chapter and getting familiar with the book's structure before picking one or two things you'd like to work on mastering.

Eventually you'll find yourself completely focused, fully aware of yourself, your partner, your opponents and the ball. Not only will your doubles game improve, you'll feel transported into the state of truly being On the Ball.

14

CHAPTER 1

Orientation

1.1 The Shot Cycle

Shot cycles are the building blocks of each point. The shot cycle* is a model that helps in understanding the many different components that make up a tennis shot.

Centering, receiving and sending are the three phases of the shot cycle. When you play a point, you alternate between receiving and sending the ball. In the interval between sending and receiving, you a have moment to center yourself. Each of the shot cycle's three phases has three parts, which are discussed in detail on the next four pages.

Centering Moment
- ready position
- clear mind
- split step

Receiving Phase
- judge the ball
- move into position
- take the racquet back

Sending Phase
- impact point (hit)
- follow-through
- recovery

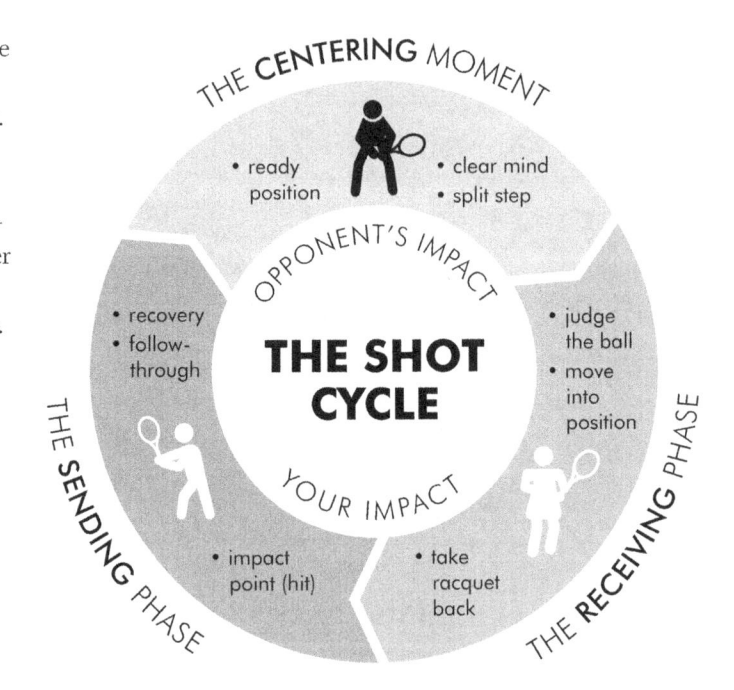

---

* The shot cycle is a core concept in the Canadian coaching system (Elderton, 2018). I've modified it to highlight the centering moment as a separate phase. Key terms, such as the shot cycle, are defined in the glossary.

The Shot Cycle | Centering moment

Every point begins with the Server centering himself before hitting the serve. After that, the centering moment occurs every time either of your opponents hits the ball. The centering moment has three parts.

Ready position
- Hold your racquet in front of your body in a neutral (continental or Eastern forehand) grip.
- Hold the racquet handle loosely with your dominant hand.
- Use your nondominant hand to support the throat of your racquet.
- The ready position for volleys is higher and farther in front of your body than for groundstrokes.

Clear mind
- Maintain an inner sense of balance, calm and readiness.
- Be mentally open to the possibility of moving in any direction.

Split step*
- Make a gentle bounce on the balls of your feet as your opponent hits the ball.
- Your split step occurs at a specific location on the court called a "home."
- The split step physically prepares you to move in any direction.

The centering moment, punctuated by the split step, is extremely important and needs to be learned and trained until it becomes automatic. Once you no longer have to think about centering, your entire game takes on the qualities of ease and spaciousness.

---

* Throughout this book I frequently use the term "split step" to refer to the entire centering moment; the ready position and a clear mind are assumed.

The Shot Cycle | Receiving from the baseline

The receiving phase begins as you finish your split step. It continues until the ball bounces on your side of the court, just before you start to swing your racquet forward. The receiving phase has three parts.

Judge the ball
- When receiving from the baseline, assess if your partner is going to take the ball as a volley or whether it will come through to you.
- Decide whether to hit a forehand or backhand.

Move into position
- From your split step, turn sideways and move toward (or sometimes away from) the ball.
- Slow down, taking smaller steps as you come closer to the ball. Keep your feet moving.
- As you focus on the ball coming toward you, momentarily expand your awareness to include where your partner and opponents are located on the court.
- Decide on other elements, such as depth, height or spin, that you'll use to manipulate your shot.

Take your racquet back
- Take the racquet back as you move into position, changing your grip if necessary.
- Breathe in as you take the racquet back.
- Have your racquet back by the time the ball bounces on the court.
- Your eyes are now completely focused on the ball.

On the court it's best to focus on one thing at a time, such as having your racquet back by the time the ball bounces. After the thing you're focusing on becomes familiar, and you no longer have to think about it, it's time to work on something else. Eventually you'll feel balanced and competent in all three phases.

The Shot Cycle | Receiving from the net

You have much less time in the receiving phase when playing from the net than baseline, as you're closer to where the opponent hits the ball, and it doesn't bounce.

Judge the ball
- Watch the opponent's body position and racquet to anticipate what sort of ball he's likely to send.
- Make a decision whether you plan to take the ball or leave it for your partner.
- Decide whether you'll hit a forehand, backhand or overhead.

Move into position
- From your split step, turn sideways and move toward the ball. You'll have time for one or two steps.
- It's especially important to move diagonally forward toward the ball when playing from the net.
- When receiving a lob, turn sideways and move into position, usually moving back.
- Decide on the intended target for your shot.

Take the racquet back
- Most volleys are hit with very little backswing.
- Unless you're hitting a swinging volley, keep the racquet in front of your body as you prepare to hit the ball.

Often, there's no time to think when receiving a volley. Once you're experienced at playing from the net, you'll discover the miraculous ability of your body to judge the ball and put the racquet in exactly the right spot.

© THOMAS KILGOUR

The Shot Cycle | Sending

The sending phase occurs between the time you start your forward swing until just before the centering moment. The sending phase has three parts.

Impact Point
- Keep your eyes focused on the ball as it bounces and moves toward you.
- The weight transfer, balance and rotation of your body all contribute to the quality of the impact.
- The path, angle and speed of your racquet at the moment of impact determines how the ball will travel and where it will land.
- Height, direction, depth, speed (also called power) and spin are the five ways the ball can be manipulated.
- Breathe out and relax your arm as you hit the ball.
- Hold the grip of your racquet firmly but without excessive tension as you make contact with the ball.

Follow-through
- After impact, the momentum of the swing on a groundstroke carries the racquet across (or sometimes on the same side of) the body.
- Most volleys have little or no follow-through.

Recovery
- After the follow-through, immediately move to an optimal place on the court, called your "home."
- As you prepare to split step, keep your feet moving.

The best place to hit the ball is in the center of the strings, called the "sweet spot." This name reflects how good it feels to hit the ball well.

1.2 Court Geography

These are some key terms you need to know to orient yourself for the remainder of the book.

Starting Positions (Chapter 2)

Every point begins with each player playing one of four Starting Positions. The exact location on the court where each player can start varies a lot.

One Up and One Back (Chapter 3)

Once a point begins, the players' starting positions dissolve as the point unfolds and a playing formation develops. Both teams playing one up and one back is the most common playing formation.

Both Up and Both Back (Chapter 4)

Both up and both back are also playing formations. When a player joins his partner at net, it's called a both-up formation. When a player joins his partner at the baseline, it's called a both-back formation.

The Homes

A home is the place on the court to which you recover by the time your opponent hits the ball. This is where the centering moment occurs.

Doubles Zones

The zones are a way of thinking about the court that directly relates to how doubles is played. I use a four-zone system that was created by Helle Sparre and is described in her book *Dynamite Doubles* (2004).

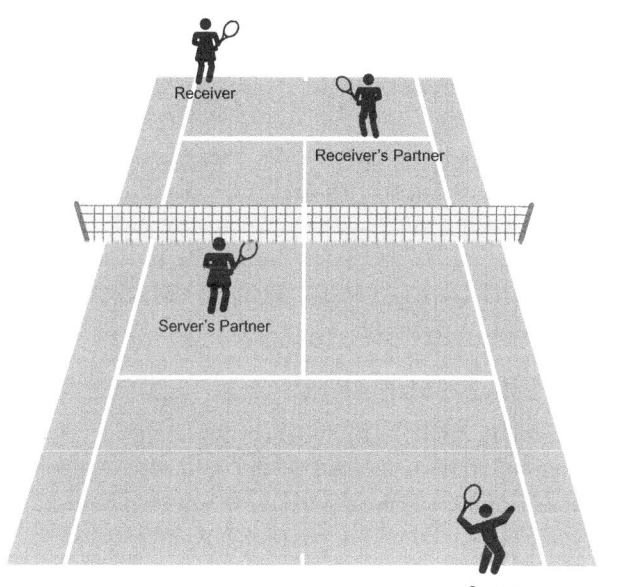

1.2.1 Every point begins with each of the four players assigned to a particular starting position. These are the standard starting locations.

Court Geography | The homes

The homes are tools to teach you where to be when your opponent hits the ball. Being at the right place for the centering moment greatly increases the likelihood that you'll reach your opponent's shot (receiving phase) and be able to hit an effective one back (sending phase).

I make a distinction between your location at the start of the point and the homes that you play from during the point. They can be, but aren't necessarily, the same place.

After the point begins, the homes are where you split step every time your opponent hits the ball. From here you may need to run a long way or just take a few small steps to receive the ball. After you hit, you recover back to your home and the shot cycle begins again.

It's important to understand the rationale behind the location of the suggested homes and learn to play from them. However, the locations of the homes aren't set in stone. As you become more experienced, you'll learn how to constantly adjust the location of your home in relation to where the ball is in the opponent's end of the court, your knowledge of where he likes to hit, and your personal shot preferences.

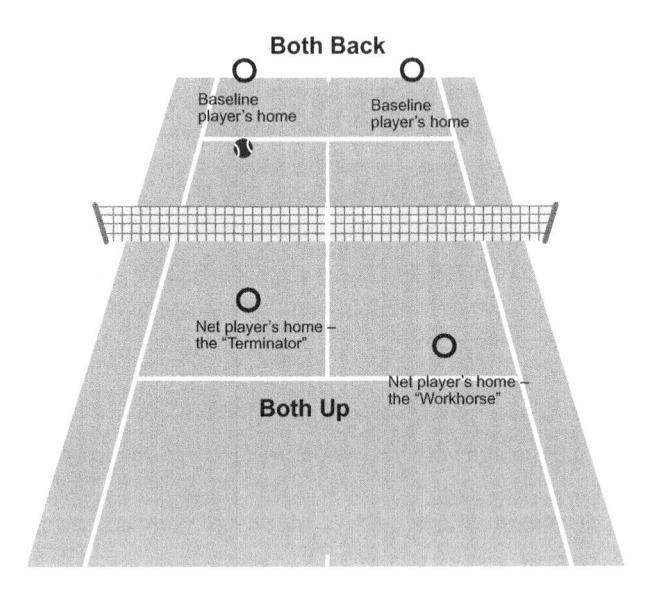

1.2.2 These are the standard homes when playing both up or both back. The homes of the both-up team are showing the "staggered offense" system (introduced in diagram 4.1.4).

Court Geography | The one-up and one-back homes

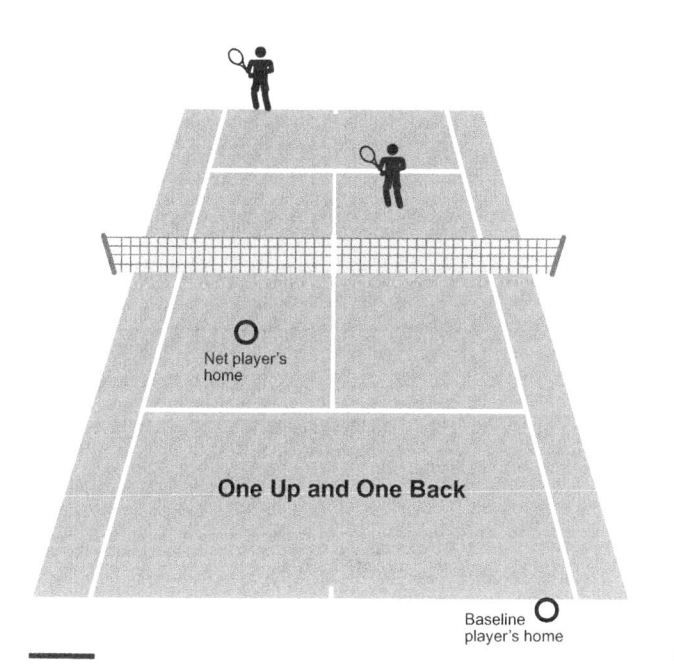

1.2.3 Standard homes when playing the one-up and one-back formation.

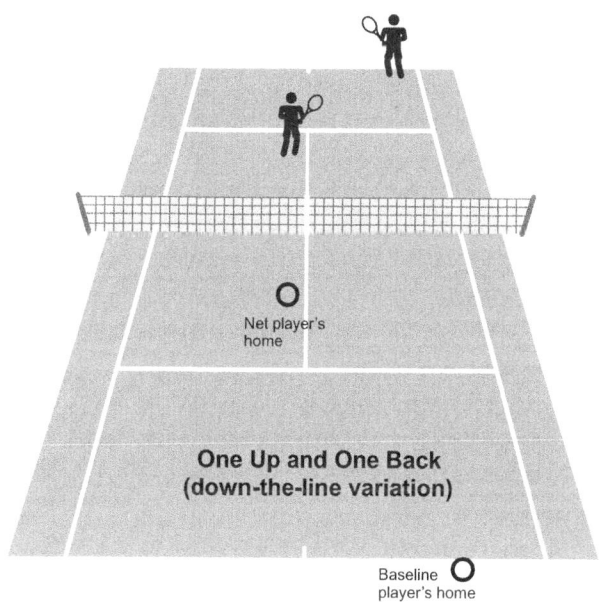

1.2.4 Standard homes when playing the down-the-line variation of the one-up and one-back formation.

Court Geography | Doubles zones

A zone is simply an area of the court that helps you orient yourself when you play.

Defense Zone
- Most of the defense zone lies outside of the lined area of the court.
- Hit groundstrokes, including drives, dipping shots and lobs, when playing from inside this zone.
- Always let the ball bounce when playing from this zone.

Transition Zone
- Move through this zone when moving from defense to offense or vice versa.
- You can hit in this zone so long as you recover to an appropriate home in the defense or offense zone.
- Avoid being in this zone as your opponent hits the ball.

Offense Zone
- Playing from this zone is known as "playing at net."
- Hit volleys, half-volleys and overheads from this zone.
- Whenever possible, hit the ball before the bounce when playing from this zone.

Attack Zone
- When you can move into the attack zone to hit a volley, you have a good chance to win the point.
- Since you're so close to the net you can hit down on the ball.
- This a one-ball zone. Recover back to the offense zone after you have hit from here.

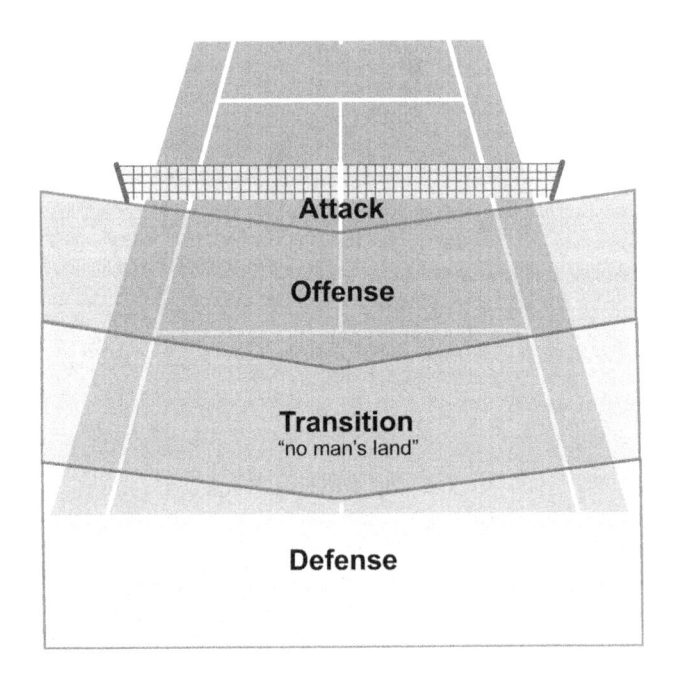

1.2.5 The zones extend well beyond the lined area to the side and back boundaries of the entire paved area of the court. While the lines are the boundaries for the balls, the entire court area is the boundary for the players. If there's no physical divider between courts you could even run into the next court to retrieve a very angled shot.

Court Geography | Guide to diagrams

This book has many diagrams. They're designed to help you integrate the text and make it easier to apply the concepts to your play. I've attempted to keep them as simple as possible, so they can be easily understood without you having to spend time deciphering them.

Note that a player's feet represent the exact location of where he's standing on the court.

Also, pay attention to the location of the ball when it's included in a diagram. The players' positions are always in relation to where the ball is on the court.

Key Symbols

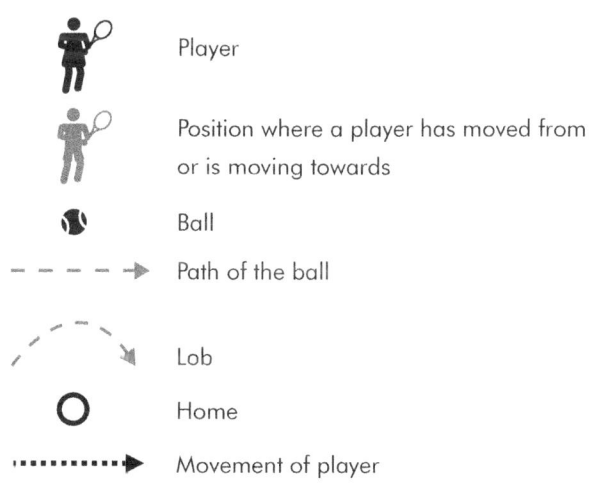

👤	Player
👤 (gray)	Position where a player has moved from or is moving towards
●	Ball
– – –▶	Path of the ball
⌒▶	Lob
○	Home
▪▪▪▪▶	Movement of player

1.2.6 In the near end of the court, the net player has moved back to protect against a possible poach. The ball is behind him. In the far court, the net player is preparing to move forward to poach the crosscourt ball being sent.

Court Geography | Bisecting the angles of return

Court geometry helps determine the best location for the homes. It also helps explain why their location changes when the ball is in different places in the opponents' end of the court.

Every time your opponent hits a ball that goes in, it will land somewhere between the two most extreme angles that could possibly be hit. The two extreme angles are called the "possible angles of return."

- Positioning yourself in the middle of these two angles at the centering moment is called "bisecting the possible angles of return."
- Understanding the angles helps locate the optimal location for each partner's home.
- In doubles, the responsibility for covering the area where the opponent can hit is shared between the two partners.

Some of the diagrams use lines to demonstrate the method of bisecting the angles of return.

Explanation of Lines

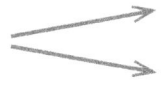

Shows the best possible angles of return

Divides the partner's responsibilities

Shows the middle of each player's area of responsibility

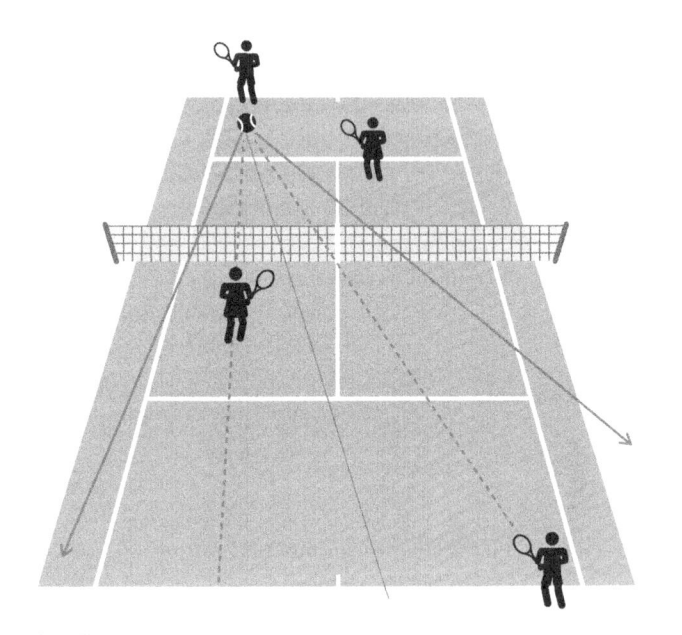

1.2.7 The baseline and net player in the near end of the court are both standing in the middle (bisecting) of their individual areas. Notice this places the baseline player close to the singles sideline. The line that divides the partners' responsibilities provides a guideline for the approximate area each partner should cover. However, there are many situations in which a player should hit a ball that's in their partner's area.

Court Geography | Lines and dimensions

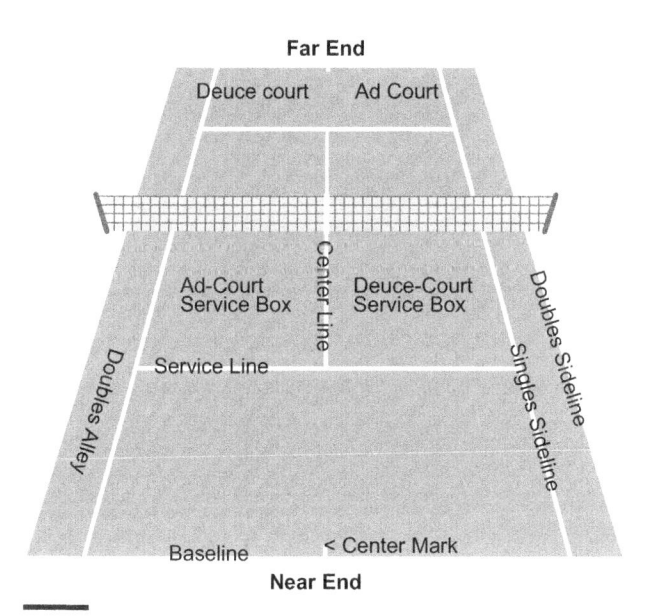

1.2.8 It helps to know the names of these lines and court areas to follow the discussion in this book. I use the terms "side" and "court" interchangeably when referring to deuce and ad. The term "end" always refers to which side of the net, that is, either the near end or the far end of the court.

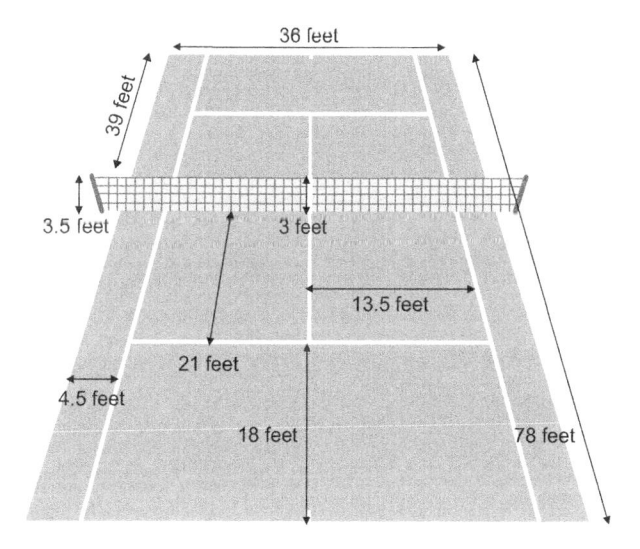

1.2.9 The court dimensions provide some interesting facts relevant to doubles. A doubles team must cover 1,404 square feet (that's 702 square feet each). A singles player must cover 1,053 square feet on his own. While a doubles player has less court to cover personally, this also means there's less open space to put the ball away in the opponent's end of the court.

28

CHAPTER 2

Starting the Point

2.1 The Four Starting Positions

Every doubles point begins with each player in one of four starting positions. All four players cycle through playing all the positions during the course of a set. Each of the starting positions must be learned and there's no way to completely avoid one you don't like. The positions are:
- Server (S)
- Server's Partner (SP)
- Receiver (R)
- Receiver's Partner (RP)

At the end of each game, the roles of Server and Server's Partner go to the opposite team and vice versa. Each player serves once before repeating the order for the rest of the set.

Within each team, either partner may serve first at the beginning of each set. Consider the skills of both the Server and the net player (Server's Partner) when deciding who will be your team's first server. Start with the strongest overall combination.

Receivers must play from the same side for the entire set. Each team chooses one player to play the deuce (right) side and the other to play the ad (left) side.

Receiver and Receiver's Partner change roles every second point as the Server alternates between serving from the deuce and ad side.

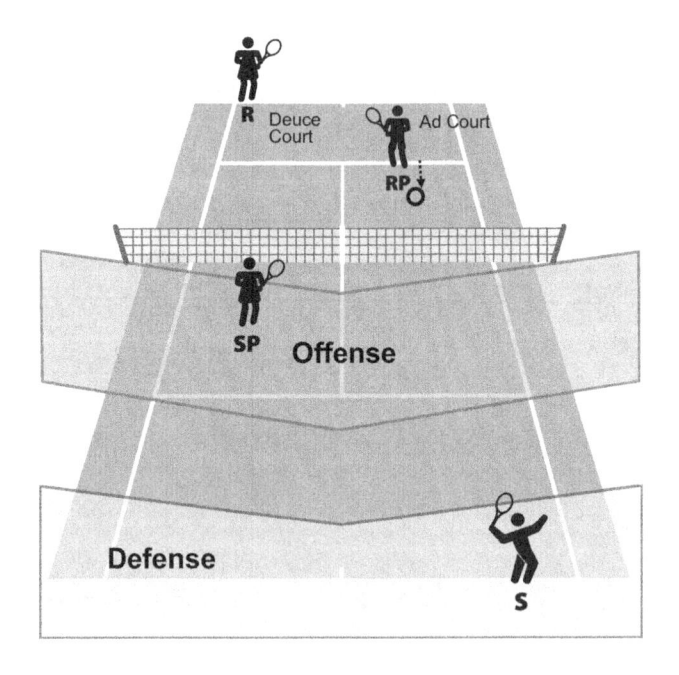

2.1.1 In the most common starting formation, the Server and Receiver start in the defense zone, and Server's Partner and Receiver's Partner start in the offense zone. Once the return of serve has passed Server's Partner, Receiver's Partner moves forward to her home in the middle of the service box (see diagram 2.6.2).

The Four Starting Positions | Starting locations vary

The rules of tennis accommodate considerable variation on where each player is allowed to start the point. This chapter covers where and why to stand in a particular place at the beginning of a point and when to make changes.

The Server must start behind the baseline, between the doubles sideline and the center mark. Receiver, Receiver's Partner and Server's Partner may start anywhere on their own side of the net, either inside or outside the lined area of the court.

Savvy players make adjustments from point to point. You can also change your starting location between the first and second serve, and you're even allowed to move while the Server is in motion.

It's important to understand that the starting location isn't necessarily the same place as the home. After the point is started with a serve and return, you move to and play from your appropriate home. The different home locations are covered in Chapters 3 and 4.

Sometimes the optimal starting location is the same as your home (for example, when Server's Partner starts in the middle of the service box). More often than not, after the point begins, you'll need to move from your starting location to your home.

2.1.2 Notice how much variation is possible in this unusual starting arrangement that could make tactical sense. By the end of this chapter you'll understand why you might start in each of these locations.

2.2 Choosing a Receiving Side

When looking for a partner, find someone who complements your weaknesses with her strengths. For example, if you're weak at net, be sure your partner is a strong net player. If you love to put the ball away but tend to be inconsistent, look for a partner who's consistent and able to hit shots to set you up.

Recreational players usually play with many different partners and must be prepared to play either the ad or deuce side. However, your game will likely improve if you choose to specialize on a side and play from it most of the time.

If you're playing with a new partner and only have a few moments to choose sides, check whether either partner has a strong preference. If not, put the stronger player on the ad side.

At one time, the sides were referred to as the "forehand" and "backhand" sides. This was based on the idea that the player with the stronger forehand groundstroke should play on the right side where she could use her crosscourt forehand, and vice versa. Of course, these terms only made sense for right-handers.

It turns out that there's a lot more to consider in choosing a side than your ability to hit forehand or backhand crosscourt groundstrokes.

2.2.1 You don't necessarily need a strong backhand to play the ad side. Some ad-court players dominate with a powerful inside-out forehand while protecting a relatively weak backhand.

Choosing a Receiving Side | Considerations

The following lists outline shots and attributes that are especially beneficial to have when playing one side or the other. Use these lists to clarify to which side you're most suited or to help you figure out which skills you want to develop. It's not expected that you'll have all the shots and attributes that relate to one side or the other.

Left-handed Players

Deuce player (forehand in middle)
- Deep crosscourt backhand
- Short-angle crosscourt backhand
- Down-the-line backhand
- Inside-out crosscourt forehand
- Lob
- Forehand volley
- Able to effectively reach angled shots to the backhand side, especially on the return of serve

Ad player (backhand in middle)
- Deep crosscourt forehand
- Short-angle crosscourt forehand
- Down-the-line forehand
- Inside-out crosscourt backhand
- Overhead
- Backhand volley
- Returns well under pressure
- Often the stronger partner
- Often the more aggressive partner
- Often the taller partner

Right-handed Players

Deuce player (backhand in middle)
- Deep crosscourt forehand
- Short-angle crosscourt forehand
- Down-the-line forehand
- Inside-out crosscourt backhand
- Lob
- Backhand volley
- Often the steadier partner
- Often the faster, more mobile partner

Ad player (forehand in the middle)
- Deep crosscourt backhand
- Short-angle crosscourt backhand
- Down-the-line backhand
- Inside-out crosscourt forehand
- Overhead
- Forehand volley
- Returns well under pressure
- Often the stronger player
- Often the more aggressive partner
- Often the taller partner

Choosing a Receiving Side | The lefty-righty team

A lefty-righty team can be formidable if they know how to capitalize on the combination. In modern doubles, the lefty usually plays the deuce side. However, both ways have advantages and disadvantages. The main consideration is whether to put the forehands or backhands in the middle.

Lefty plays the deuce court
- Both forehands are in the middle, making for strong poaching opportunities for both teammates.
- Teams that like to play both up at net will benefit from having the lefty play on the deuce court.
- It can more difficult for opponents to hit a winning ball through the middle.

Lefty plays the ad court
- Both backhands are in the middle. Both players need strong backhand volleys to ensure effective poaching.
- It can be easier for opponents to hit a winning ball through the middle.
- Both forehands are on the outside, which for most players is an advantage at the baseline.
- Both partners need to develop their inside-out backhand returns to be effective with this arrangement.

2.2.2 As a lefty playing on the deuce side, you'll need to be able to return the angled serve with your backhand while avoiding a poach from Server's Partner's forehand volley. The natural spin of a right-handed server makes the ball curve away from you and a slice serve will intensify this effect.

2.3 The Server

When the serving team wins a game, it's said that they've "held serve." To execute a good serve it's of prime importance to relax your mind and body, especially your serving arm. The main job of the Server is to begin the point by getting the serve over the net and into the diagonal service box in the opponent's end. A secondary job is to call out the score before each point.

The first point of a game is always started from the deuce (right) side of the court. Points alternate from ad (left) to deuce after that and so on. The Server gets two attempts on every point. If you miss both serves, it's called a double fault and you lose the point. Ideally, at least 75 percent of your first serves should go in.

Mixing up the placement, spin, depth and power of your serves puts pressure on the Receiver. A serve that challenges the Receiver may lead to a weak return that your partner can put away from the net.

The serve is unique in that is has no receiving phase; in fact, it's the only time where you get to put the ball exactly where you want. Ideally you set the service toss up straight, in front of your body and slightly higher than you can reach with your racquet in hand. If you make a poor toss, you're allowed to re-toss as long as you haven't hit it. It makes good sense to discipline yourself to re-do bad tosses.

2.3.1 The Server must start from behind the baseline, anywhere between the doubles sideline and the center mark. You may not step on or over the baseline or cross to the other side of the center mark until after you have hit the ball. The usual starting location is about halfway between the doubles sideline and center mark. The service motion usually carries the Server a step or two into the court after impact. Immediately recover to your home behind the baseline to be ready for the return.

The Server | The serve ritual

The serve ritual is a series of steps you do before every serve to help you stay calm and focused. Add your own personal touches to make it meaningful to you.

1. Walk to your starting position, taking care to check the position of your feet behind the baseline. Call out the score.
2. Decide where and how (for example, with spin or flat, serve and volley) you want to serve.*
3. Take a full inhale and exhale. While taking this breath you can silently repeat a positive phrase, such as "I've got this" or "Trust yourself."
4. Do something to help you narrow your focus. Most players bounce the ball a set number of times before beginning their service motion.
5. Find a way to keep your mind occupied during your service motion so that the body can do what it knows how to do. For example:
- Focus on inhaling on your wind-up and toss, and exhaling on your hit and follow-through.
- Feel the extension of the arm making your toss.
- Silently repeat a key phrase, such as "Reach up."

---

* If you're telling your partner where you intend to serve by talking between points, you'll need to communicate where you intend to place both your serves before moving to your starting location. This reverses steps one and two.

The Serve Ritual

- Check your feet. Call the score.
- Decide where to place your serve.
- Take a full inhale and exhale.
- Narrow your focus.
- Keep your mind occupied.

• Take Your Time
• Make It Repeatable
• Make It Relevant

The Server | Placing the serve

Placing the serve is the act of deliberately sending your serve toward a particular area within the service box. This is one way you can make your serve more effective once you have the ability to get it in. *Depth* and *direction* are the two aspects of placement.

Depth refers to how far forward or back in the service box the serve lands. Serves that land deep (in the back half or third of the service box) are generally more difficult for the Receiver than shorter serves. Sometimes a serve that lands short can pose a challenge for the Receiver, especially if it comes as a surprise.

Direction refers to how close to the sideline or center line the serve lands. The T, body and angled serves are the three serve directions.

The T serve lands close to the center line and gets its name from the shape made where the center line meets the service line. The body serve (B) is hit toward the Receiver's body and is intended to jam her. The angled serve* (A) travels toward the sideline and can be effective hit either short or deep. It's even more potent hit with slice and works well as a surprise tactic.

---

* The angled serve is sometimes called the wide serve. For the sake of clarity, I don't use this term as "wide" also refers to a ball that lands outside of the service box's sideline.

2.3.2 The T serve is the go-to serve in doubles. It helps set your partner up at net, especially when hit to the backhand side of the Receiver. The body serve is best hit with spin or power and works especially well against tall players. The angled serve must be used with caution, especially when hit to the Receiver's forehand side. On the angled serve, the Server must be ready to sprint forward to cover a short-angle return, which is a likely response.

The Server | Adding spin

Spin refers to the way the ball spins as it travels through the air. It's created by using a brushing motion as the racquet strikes the ball. Adding spin to your serve can improve your consistency and increase the difficulty for the Receiver. A continental grip and racquet head speed are needed to create spin.

Slice serve
- The racquet brushes across the right side of the ball.
- The ball curves to the left as it travels towards the opponent's end.
- Viewed from the Receiver's end, the ball curves to the right.
- A slice serve works well to pull your opponent out wide on the deuce side or to jam the ball into her body.

Topspin serve
- The racquet brushes across the top of the ball and travels higher over the net than either a flat or slice serve.
- A topspin serves adds difficulty by kicking up after it lands.

Topspin-slice serve
- A topspin-slice combination brushes across the top right side of the ball.
- This gives you the advantages of the net clearance of topspin with some of the curve of the slice.

2.3.3 Many players learn to serve using a forehand grip because in the beginning it's the easiest way to get the ball in. When you first change to the continental grip, it will probably feel foreign and the ball will travel in an unexpected direction. Trust that becoming comfortable with spin will eventually give you a more reliable serve.

The Server | The left-handed server

All players need to adjust when faced with a serve hit by a left-hander. It's challenging because it's less familiar as righties and lefties alike aren't faced with left-handers very often. The natural curve of a left-handed serve is to the right, opposite to that of a right-handed serve. If you're left-handed, adding spin to your serve can give you a great weapon.

Slice serve
- The racquet brushes across the left side of the ball.
- The ball curves to the right as it travels towards the opponent's end.
- Viewed from the Receiver's end, the ball curves to the left.
- A slice serve curves to the backhand side of the right-handed Receiver. This is especially challenging on the ad side.

Topspin serve
- A pure topspin serve is similar to that of a right-handed Server.
- The racquet brushes across the top of the ball, which kicks up after it lands.

Topspin-slice serve
- The racquet brushes across the top, left side of the ball.
- This serve adds difficulty for the Receiver by kicking up toward her backhand side.

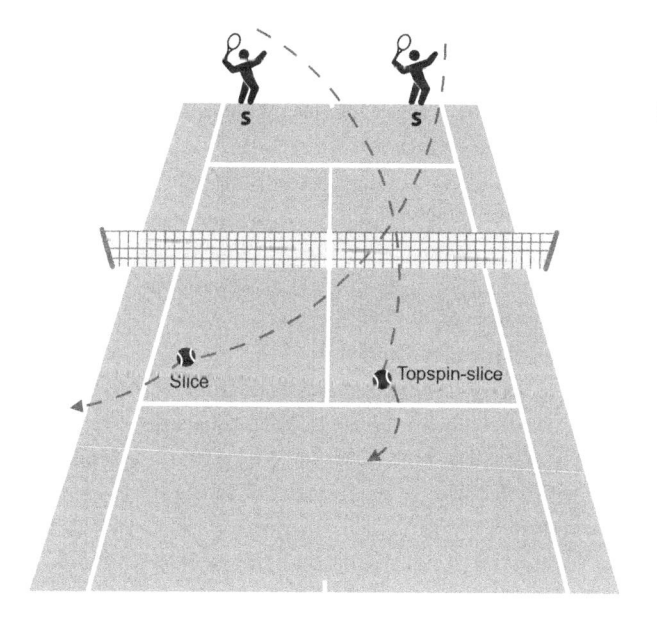

2.3.4 When you add spin to your serve as left-hander, it bounces in the opposite direction to that of a right-handed server. It usually takes awhile for the Receiver to adjust, especially in doubles where you only serve once every four games.

The Server | Serve and volley

The serve and volley is a tactic that's planned before the Server begins the point. After serving, you immediately run toward the net, ready to volley the return. This places you up at net with your partner in the both-up formation.

Serve and volley was once commonplace in both singles and doubles. Its use has declined as changing racquet and string technology has dramatically improved players' returns and the ability to pass the net player.

Even so, the serve and volley has a place in modern doubles. It's used at least some of the time by both men and women, from about the NTRP 3.5 level up.

- With two players to cover the court, there's less space for the Receiver to make a successful return than in singles.
- Teams who prefer to play both up use it to get both players into the net right away.
- Even if you don't serve and volley all the time, using it occasionally challenges the Receiver to adapt.

For further information on serve and volley, see diagrams 4.2.7 and 5.5.2–5.5.4.

2.3.5 The serve and volley tactic is more common on a first serve than a second. Knowing she has a back-up, the Server has more freedom to hit a serve that will challenge the Receiver. Depth, direction and spin are the recommended ways to add challenge when using the serve and volley. Increasing the speed is not recommended as it gives you less time to get into the net and the return may come back faster as well.

The Server | First and second serves

Once you have the ability to do something more with your serve than just get it in the box, it's time to create a difference between your first and second serve. Or, if you have a huge difference between your first and second serve, consider backing off on your first serve and/or strengthening your second.

On your first serve you have a backup, so you can afford to take some risk to make it more difficult for the Receiver and increase the likelihood of setting up your partner for a poach. Keep in mind the general guideline of getting in 75 percent of your first serves.

On the second serve, you want to get the ball in (ideally, 100 percent of the time) without giving the Receiver the opportunity to win or gain control of the point. You should only be using your second serve one out of four points, so you'll need to develop and gain confidence with your second serve in practice, outside of match play.

The First Serve

- Focus on hitting serves that are likely to set up your partner to poach. Power, spin or placement can all be effective.
- Hit most first serves to the Receiver's weaker side. Occasionally, hit to the other side or into her body.
- Consider using the serve and volley.
- If you never miss a first serve, take more risk. Find a way to make your first serve more effective.
- On an important point, such as a game point or every point in a tiebreak, get your first serve in by using the serve with which you're most comfortable. You still want to relax and hit freely. For example, you could hit in your favorite direction or add extra spin.

The Second Serve

- Take your time. Use the same serve ritual as on your first serve.
- Aim to hit deep, while still keeping the ball in, and toward the Receiver's weaker side.
- Use topspin or topspin-slice to provide increased net clearance while improving your chance of keeping the ball in.
- If you currently just get your second serve in the box, figure out where you're most comfortable placing the ball. Work on making this serve completely reliable, so you can hit it with confidence even when you're under pressure.
- Don't serve and volley unless you're very competent using this tactic.
- Be especially mindful to recover to the correct baseline home because the Receiver is more likely to hit a strong return from your second serve.

The Server | Key points

Receiving Phase
- The serve is the only shot where there's no receiving phase. It begins with centering and ends in the sending phase.

Centering Moment
- The serve ritual helps prepare and center the Server.
- The centering "moment" is actually a few seconds as the Server takes her time to get centered.
- The Server provides the setup for the serve with the service toss. Developing a consistent toss is essential.

Sending Phase
- The first and second serve should differ. A reliable second serve gives you the confidence to take more risk on the first serve.
- Learning to place your serve with direction and depth makes your serve much more effective.
- Once you have developed a solid serve with the correct grip and good racquet head speed, adding spin can take your serve to another level.
- If you're left-handed, learning to use spin on your serve is well worth the effort, as your opponents must adapt to your serve curving in an unfamiliar direction.
- If you've stepped or jumped into the court after your serve, be sure to recover to your home behind the baseline by the time your opponent hits the return.

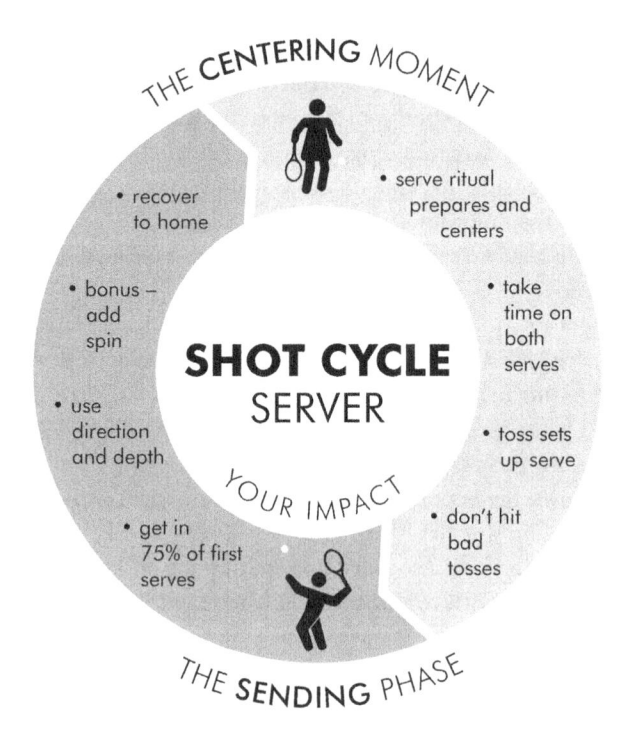

SHOT CYCLE SERVER

THE CENTERING MOMENT
- serve ritual prepares and centers
- take time on both serves
- toss sets up serve
- don't hit bad tosses

YOUR IMPACT

THE SENDING PHASE
- get in 75% of first serves
- use direction and depth
- bonus – add spin
- recover to home

2.4 Server's Partner

Strong, consistent volleys and knowing when to poach* are key attributes of Server's Partner.

The main job of Server's Partner is to put pressure on the receiving team through effective net play, especially poaching balls that travel through the middle and putting away any short balls.

The standard starting location of Server's Partner is the center of the service box, although you're allowed to start anywhere on the court.

Server's Partner needs to be active at net and to move diagonally forward rather than sideways when poaching. You can also be active by pretending to move, called "faking."

It's important to find a balance between being active and going for shots without making unforced errors. If you're making a lot of errors you need to back off, as it's difficult for your team to hold serve if you make more than one net error in a game.

In particular, notice and adjust if you're making errors attempting to poach balls that are too low, high, or far away, especially on your backhand side. If you're frequently getting passed down the alley, you're probably leaving your alley vulnerable by moving toward the middle too soon.

2.4.1 Server's Partner usually starts in the center of the service box. You might start at the baseline if you're uncomfortable at net or if the Receiver is winning points hitting directly at you.

---

* To poach is to intercept the crosscourt ball that the opposing Receiver has directed to your partner. It can also be referred to as "cutting off" the crosscourt ball.

Server's Partner | Support the server in between points

The serving game is won or lost by the serving team, not just the Server. In addition to doing your job during the point, part of your role as Server's Partner is to support your partner in between points.
- Keep track of the score so you can help if needed.
- Conserve your partner's energy and show support by walking back to meet the Server near the baseline.
- If you're not talking between points, make frequent eye contact and verbally encourage your partner.
- In general, let the Server make decisions about serve placement or use of plays. Offer suggestions if asked.
- Be encouraging if your partner is serving poorly. Don't show frustration even if you feel it.

The Server has a big job to do starting the point. Help out by managing the balls.
- Be sure the Server has two balls to start each point and hold the third ball if requested.
- Clear first serves that your partner hits into the net.
- Keep the Server safe from balls rolling back from the fence or curtain by paying attention and alerting her if there's any danger.
- Keep track of all three balls. Notice if a ball travels into another court and take the initiative to get it back at an appropriate time.

Server's Partner can help the Server relax. The most important thing is to be positive and encouraging.

Server's Partner | Starting location

2.4.2 As Server's Partner, when you start from the center of the service box, you're slightly favoring covering the middle over covering the alley. This gives you more access to poaching and puts pressure on the Receiver to hit an accurate crosscourt return or attempt the more difficult down-the-line return. (See diagram 1.2.7 for an explanation of the solid and dotted lines used here.)

2.4.3 Some players prefer to start farther back and move in at the sound of the serve. This movement pattern can help you time your split step and be more active as Server's Partner. It may also discourage a lob return by making it look like you're playing from a position farther back than you really are.

Server's Partner | Covering the alley on an angled serve

Many players put too much emphasis on covering the alley. Unless the Receiver is regularly and consistently winning points down the alley, focus on poaching middle balls.

On an angled serve, cover the alley by moving one or two steps toward the singles sideline to adapt to the changing angles available to the Receiver.

- Don't get too close to the singles sideline. It leaves too much court for your partner to cover.
- Turn your body slightly sideways to face the ball and make it easier to reach a down-the-alley shot.
- Remember the length of your racquet and your arm outstretched will reach a considerable distance.

As the Receiver hits the ball, split step and be mentally ready to play a ball on either side. If the Receiver looks unbalanced, or is running forward, she's not likely to hit down your alley.

Pay attention to whether your opponent can hit a down-the-alley return off an angled serve. Some players won't ever attempt this shot from their backhand side. If this is the case, focus on covering the middle ball until your opponent proves she can consistently hit a down-the-alley return.

2.4.4 For most players, the forehand is easier than the backhand down-the-alley return, as shown here. However, if you're playing against a left-handed Receiver playing on the ad side, her forehand will be on the outside. Be ready for the down-the-alley return when you're playing Server's Partner on the deuce side.

Server's Partner | Covering the alley on a T serve

It's a well-known principle that T serves provide poaching opportunities for Server's Partner. While this holds some truth, be aware that many Receivers can consistently return a T serve down the alley, especially when hitting from the forehand side.

As Server's Partner on a T serve, stay at your regular location in the center of the service box. This puts you in the center of the two possible angles of the Receiver's return. Notice that this location no longer favors covering the middle over covering the alley (see diagram 2.4.2). Be ready to move diagonally forward to intercept a return hit down the alley.

If you plan to poach, wait until just before the Receiver strikes the ball before moving diagonally forward to cut-off the crosscourt ball.

Pay attention to both of the Receivers' tendencies over the course of a match and learn whether they like to return the T serve down the alley. Be especially alert when playing a left-handed Receiver playing on the deuce side. Don't be surprised when she whips her forehand down your alley off the T serve.

2.4.5 On a T serve, be mentally ready to poach or cover your alley. Be ready for the down-the-alley return if the Receiver is well set-up and hitting from her forehand side.

Server's Partner | The fake

The fake is a pretend poach by Server's Partner, designed to unsettle the Receiver and trick her into hitting a down-the-alley shot that you'll be right there to cover.

To fake, lean toward the middle as if you're going to poach just before the ball bounces on the Receiver's side. Make your move early enough so the Receiver sees you. You don't need to make your fake too big for it to be noticed. As the Receiver hits the ball, re-center your body and split step, ready for a down-the-alley return.

The fake works best when the Receiver regularly hits down the alley or directly at you. In fact, it's one way to disrupt a Receiver who's winning points with down-the-line shots.

It's difficult to poach after you have faked because your momentum takes you back toward the sideline, whereas on a poach you need to move diagonally forward.

- Use the fake occasionally on a first serve. Most of the time you'll be looking to poach and therefore won't want to fake.
- Use the fake often on a second serve, which generally offers less opportunity for poaching.

2.4.6 It's gratifying when your fake works and you volley the Receiver's down-the-alley return between the two opponents for a winner. You may be surprised how well your fake works. Be ready so you don't get tricked by your own trick.

Server's Partner | Dealing with powerful returns

2.4.7 Some Receivers will hit powerful returns directly at Server's Partner. Be ready, stand your ground, and use a volley without any swing to block the ball straight back toward the Receiver. If that's not working, move back to the baseline, perhaps only for the second serve if that's when you're getting nailed.

2.4.8 Moving back to the service line is not the answer if you feel intimidated by a hard-hitting Receiver. As you move farther back, the lateral distance to cover your half of the court increases, you become vulnerable to dipping shots hit at your feet, and it's also harder to block the ball back over the net because the net is farther away.

Server's Partner | Key points

Centering Moment
- The standard starting location is the middle of the service box.
- Split step as the Receiver hits the return.
- Depending on where the serve is heading, you may need to move a step to the left or right for your split step.
- Be sure your racquet is in the correct ready position, slightly higher and farther in front than on groundstrokes.
- Always be mentally ready to move either left or right, to cover the alley or to move toward the middle to poach.

Receiving Phase
- Develop the key skill of anticipating when you can poach.
- You have more or less time to react to a ball depending on the speed of the return.
- Most of the time the return will go to your partner rather than you. You're still in the receiving phase until your partner hits her shot.

Sending Phase
- Hit volleys and overheads when playing Server's Partner.
- How and where to hit the ball will be covered in section 3.2, "The Net Player."

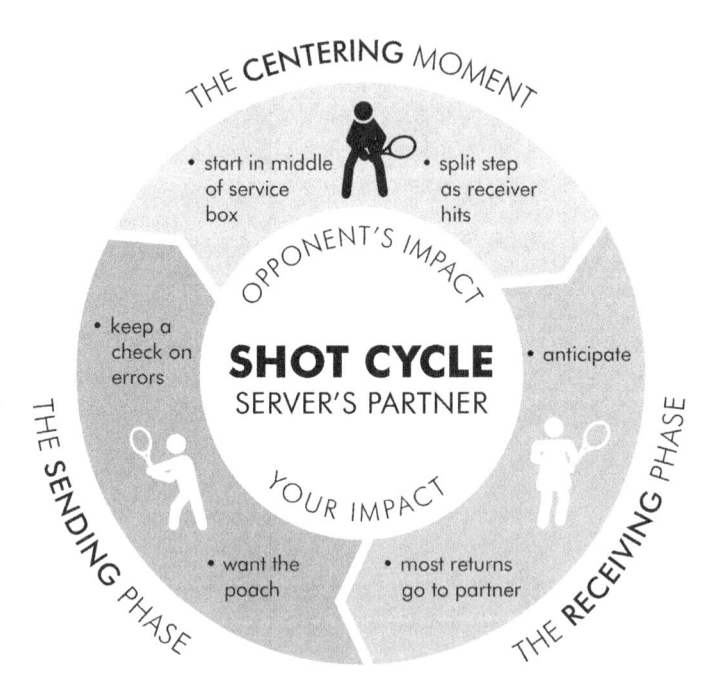

SHOT CYCLE — SERVER'S PARTNER

THE CENTERING MOMENT
- start in middle of service box
- split step as receiver hits

OPPONENT'S IMPACT

THE RECEIVING PHASE
- anticipate
- most returns go to partner

YOUR IMPACT

THE SENDING PHASE
- want the poach
- keep a check on errors

2.5 The Receiver

A consistent return of serve and the ability to respond to many different types of serves underpins good doubles play. When the Receiving team wins a game, it's said that they've "broken serve."

The main job of the Receiver is to get the ball in play, ideally keeping it away from Server's Partner. The rules of tennis doubles state that you must return from the same side (either deuce or ad) for an entire set.

The Receiver's starting location is usually close to the singles sideline, but there's a wide variation, as we shall see. The rules allow you to start anywhere on your end of the court and the ball must bounce before you hit.

As Receiver, think about where you intend to hit the return before the Server hits her serve, considering both your forehand and backhand sides. The majority of returns, 80 percent or more, should be hit crosscourt.

When Server's Partner is active at net, once every game or two, hit a down-the-line shot (called a "specialty shot") that you're confident you can make.

In doubles there's less space to hit into than in singles because Server's Partner can cover more than half of the court from her position at net (see diagram 3.2.2). Therefore, the Receiver shouldn't try to hit a winner off the return. Immediately recover to a correct home after you hit your return (see diagram 2.5.4).

2.5.1 The majority of returns should be hit crosscourt, keeping the ball well away from Server's Partner. Aim your return within the singles sideline to reduce the amount of angle that can be hit back to you.

The Receiver | Be a good sport

The Receiver is required to play at the reasonable pace of the Server.
- Make an effort to be ready when the Server steps up to the baseline.
- If the Server serves before you're ready (called a "quick serve"), you can ask that the serve is replayed as long as you have made no attempt to hit the return.

As Receiver, be prepared to call "out" any ball that lands outside the service box.
- Receiver's Partner usually calls the serves that land past the service line.
- The Receiver has a good view to call the center line. Receiver's Partner can help if she sees the ball clearly.
- As Receiver, always call the outside line as your partner has an unreliable view.

Etiquette point: The Receiver shouldn't return a first serve that's an obvious fault on a first serve as it slows down play. However, you should return a first serve that's close to the line while you're waiting for your partner to make the call.

When a player on the receiving team or an outside influence causes a long delay between first and second serves, the receiving team should award the Server two serves.

2.5.2 The Receiver has by far the clearest view to call the outside line while Receiver's Partner has the best view to call the service line.

The Receiver | Starting location

The most important thing the Receiver can do on every return is to be alert and present, making a split step at the moment the Server hits the ball.

To find your optimal starting location, stand with one foot on the singles sideline and the other on the baseline. Your body will naturally be at the correct angle facing the Server. From this location there are many variations.

- Against a left-handed Server, take a lateral step to the left to account for the difference in the natural curve of the serve.
- As Receiver, adjust your starting location based on your personal preferences. For example, move laterally to the left to protect your backhand.
- If you like to hit the return early, start a step or two in from the baseline.
- Some Receivers prefer to start farther back and move in as the Server makes her service motion, split stepping on the serve's impact.
- As Receiver, constantly adjust your starting location in response to the tendencies of the Server. For example, start two or three steps behind the baseline against a powerful serve.

2.5.3 As soon as you decide whether you'll be using your forehand or backhand, get turned and move toward, or sometimes away, from the ball. Avoid running into the ball. Remember that the serve may be traveling toward you very quickly.

The Receiver | Starting location varies

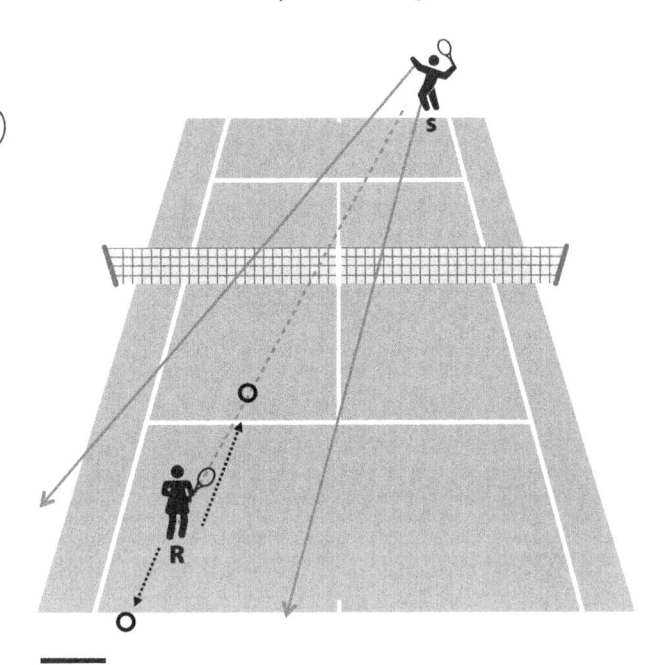

2.5.4 Take the opportunity to change your starting location between the first and second serves. Move in closer in anticipation of a weaker second serve (as shown), or move laterally to one side to increase the chance of returning the second serve from your favorite side. After your impact, recover forward or backward to an appropriate home.

2.5.5 If you prefer to return from your forehand side, move laterally to the left. This leaves the Server little space to hit to your backhand, although you need to be ready to sprint diagonally forward to reach an angled serve. After you hit the return, recover to your home near the singles sideline.

The Receiver | Hit most returns crosscourt

Hit about 80 percent of your returns crosscourt, hitting high enough or angled enough so that Server's Partner can't poach your return.

Deep crosscourt
- The deep-crosscourt shot is your go-to return when the Server stays back after her serve.
- Hit the ball into the deep-crosscourt triangle to put pressure on the Server and possibly set up your partner at net.
- This can be hit from both an inside* and outside* ball.

Short-angle crosscourt
- The short-angle crosscourt return works well against players who have difficulty moving forward.
- It's a good response to a serve and volley, as the ball will land at the Server's feet.
- The short-angle crosscourt return is easier to hit from an outside ball, when the serve lands near the sideline and isn't too deep.
- It's difficult, though not impossible, from an inside ball.

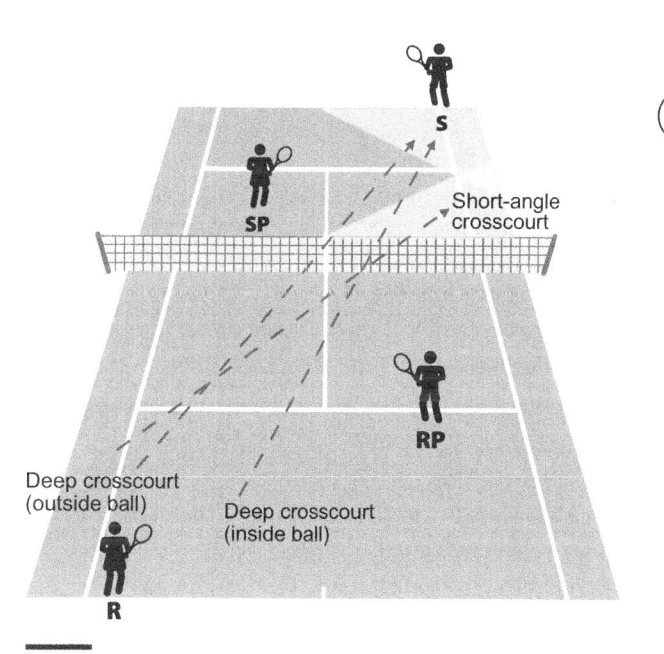

---

* An inside ball doesn't cross your body as it goes toward your racquet and is usually hit from near the middle of the court. An outside ball travels across your body as it goes toward your racquet and is usually hit from closer to the side boundary of the court.

2.5.6 Experiment with hitting a variety of crosscourt returns. Aim your return within the singles lines to reduce the amount of angle the opposing baseline player can hit on her next shot. These shots apply on both the ad and deuce sides.

The Receiver | Other crosscourt returns

There are two more crosscourt returns that can be useful in addition to the deep crosscourt and short-angle returns.

Down-the-middle crosscourt
- The down-the-middle crosscourt return is effective when hit with power, traveling low over the net.
- This shot is more advanced as it requires both power and good placement.
- It's less likely to be poached when the net player's backhand is on the inside.
- It's especially effective when playing a righty-lefty team where the backhands are in the middle.

Low-crosscourt lob
- The low-crosscourt lob is a good defensive technique on a challenging outside ball.
- This isn't an advanced shot. It's mostly a matter of remembering to use it at the right time.
- Aim this shot just high enough to keep it out of reach of Server's Partner.
- Remember to use the low crosscourt lob if your returns are frequently being poached.
- This shot isn't effective against a serve and volley as it sets the Server up nicely for her first volley.

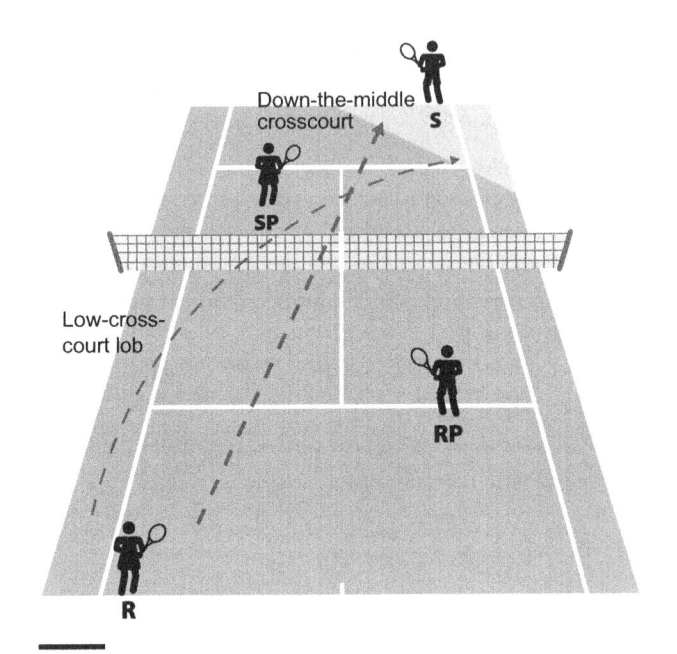

2.5.7 The low-crosscourt lob is a great defensive shot that gets you out of trouble on a difficult angled serve. Lift it up just high enough to keep it out of reach of Server's Partner. These shots apply on both the ad and deuce sides.

The Receiver | Deuce-side specialty shots

A specialty shot is a down-the-line shot you hit to avoid an active net player.

Precision down the line (inside and outside)
- The precision down the line is aimed into the alley.
- It works well when the net player moves toward the middle to poach.
- It's effective and relatively easy to hit from an outside ball on the forehand side if the serve isn't too difficult.
- The precision inside-backhand is less common and therefore not expected by the opponents.

Power shot at the net player
- This shot is hit with power toward the opposing net player.
- It may unsettle the opposing net player and reduce her overall effectiveness.
- It's equally effective from the deuce or ad side.

Lob over the net player
- The lob over the net player is especially effective on the deuce side because it travels over and lands on the backhand side of your opponents.
- A defensive lob (hit with a blocking action, similar to a volley) is effective against a powerful serve.
- Try to discreetly warn your partner if you plan to lob so she's ready to defend if your lob is short.

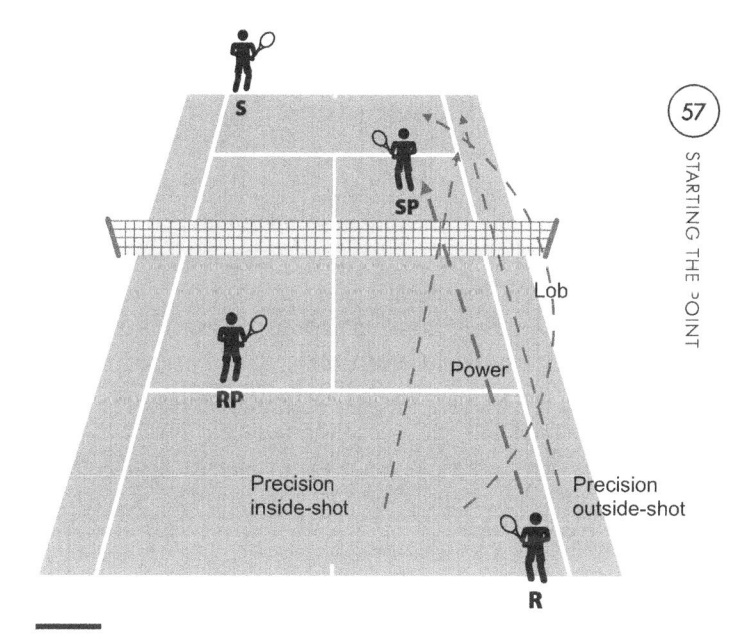

2.5.8 You don't need to develop all the different shots. Just choose your most natural one on both the forehand and backhand sides. If you're left-handed, you'll probably want to develop your precision inside-shot on your forehand side. On your backhand side, putting in the time to learn a precision down-the-line shot is an option to deal with angled serves.

The Receiver | Ad-side specialty shots

Use your specialty shots about 20 percent of the time. The majority of returns should be hit crosscourt. Except for a defensive lob, don't use these shots when you're in trouble. Wait until you're in a good position as all these shots carry more risk than a crosscourt return.

Precision down the line (inside and outside)
- This works well when the net player moves toward the middle to poach.
- The precision backhand hit from the outside is a great shot if you can hit it reliably.
- The inside precision shot hit down the line from the forehand side is relatively easy to control and is effective as long as you don't become predictable by hitting it too often.

Power shot at the net player
- This shot is hit with power directly toward the net player.
- Use it with discernment when playing against weaker players.
- It's worth developing this shot if you have a powerful forehand or backhand.

Lob over the net player
- The lob from ad side is less effective than on the deuce side as it travels over and lands on the forehand side of the opponents.
- A crosscourt lob is safer if you're using it defensively.

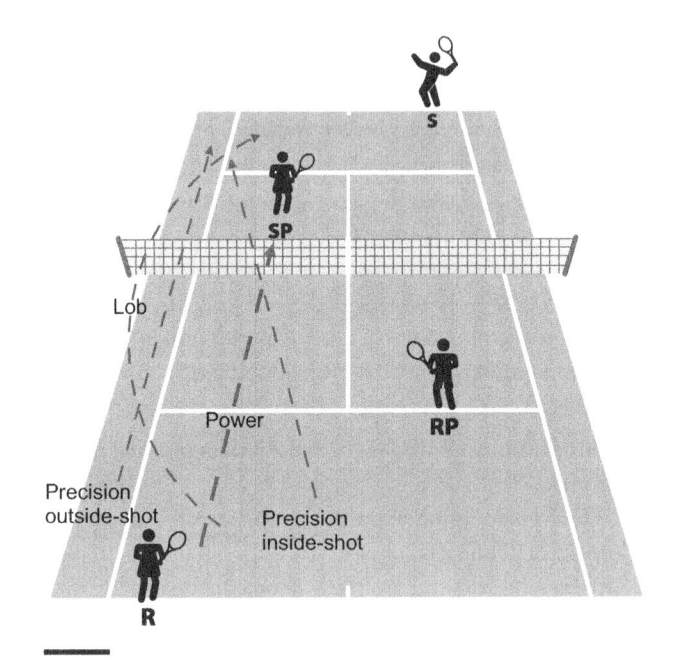

2.5.9 The precision down-the-line forehand is a good option if you're left-handed and playing from the ad side. The Server's Partner may forget that your forehand is on the outside, especially at the beginning of a match.

The Receiver | The short serve

A short serve can be surprisingly difficult to return. Think of it as no different than any other short ball. As soon as you realize that the serve will be short, run quickly forward, slowing down before the ball bounces.

If the Server regularly serves short (for example, a habitually short second serve), start farther up so you don't have to run forward to hit the return.

Be careful not to hit this return long. When you're hitting from closer to the net, the amount of distance you have available for your shot is less, perhaps by 18 feet or more.

Stay alert if the Server mixes it up, sometimes hitting hard and other times soft. When you're pre-planning where you're going to hit the return, include an option for the short serve.

- If you can hit a crosscourt drop-shot or power at the net player return, go for it.
- Otherwise, don't try anything fancy or expect to make a winner off the return.
- A good option is to return crosscourt and follow it into the net (see diagram 4.2.5).
- Run around to hit the ball on your favorite side (forehand or backhand) whenever possible.
- Use topspin to keep the ball in.
- Use slice to help control the ball and keep it low.

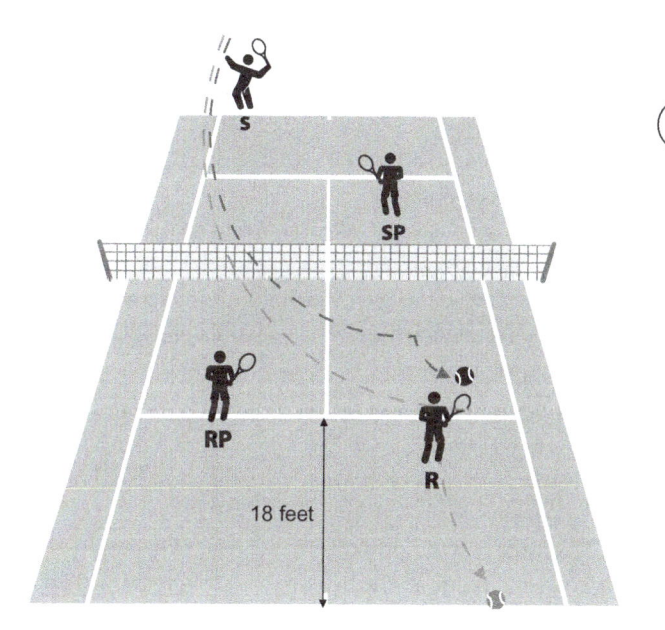

2.5.10 There are few things more frustrating in tennis than repeatedly missing a soft, short serve. First you hit one long, the next you dump into the net and then it's in your head. If you're having trouble, you need to find a way to get the ball back and use the short serve to your advantage.

The Receiver | Key points

Centering Moment
- Plan your intended target for a forehand or backhand return before the Server hits her serve.
- The key to returning well is to be present when the Server hits her serve.
- The split step is especially important on the return of serve because you're responding to a fast moving ball.
- Choose and adjust your starting location based on the Server's tendencies and your personal preferences.

Receiving Phase
- The return of serve is the only shot that must bounce before you hit it.
- As soon as you decide whether to hit a forehand or backhand get turned. (It's the reTURN.)
- Use your perception skills to move quickly in the correct direction. The ball may be moving toward you quickly. Avoid running into it.
- Against a powerful serve, use a shorter backswing.

Sending Phase
- Hit your return crosscourt 80 percent of the time.
- Get the ball over the net and in play.
- Develop confidence and consistency with four different speciality shots: one on the forehand and one on the backhand for the deuce and ad sides.
- Immediately recover to an appropriate home after you hit your return.

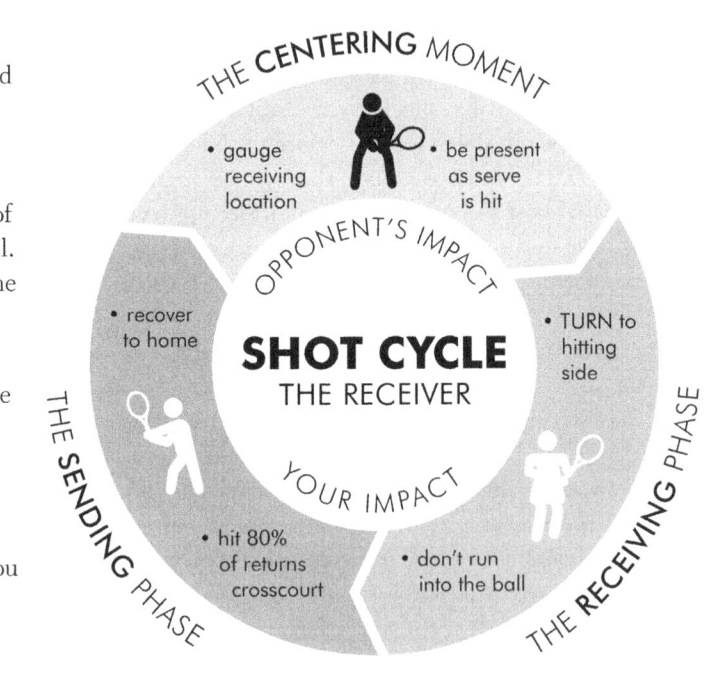

SHOT CYCLE — THE RECEIVER

THE CENTERING MOMENT
- gauge receiving location
- be present as serve is hit

OPPONENT'S IMPACT

THE RECEIVING PHASE
- TURN to hitting side
- don't run into the ball

YOUR IMPACT

THE SENDING PHASE
- hit 80% of returns crosscourt
- recover to home

2.6 Receiver's Partner

The Receiver's Partner's* position is nicknamed the "hot seat." You're vulnerable to a poaching attack by Server's Partner because your opponent's strong serve may lead to a weak return by your partner.

When playing Receiver's Partner, your main job is to defend a poach by Server's Partner. Your secondary job is to call "out" any ball that lands beyond the service line.

Receiver's Partner usually starts on or just behind the service line, halfway between the center line and singles sideline. Face the opposite net player rather than turning your body sideways to watch the service line. From here you're well situated to defend a poach hit by Server's Partner and also in good position to move closer to net after the danger from Server's Partner has passed.

There's a specific procedure for Receiver's Partner that details where to focus your gaze, how to defend, and where and when to move forward. Many players play the Receiver's Partner position badly because they don't follow this procedure. This is a pity because it's not that difficult to learn and execute.

2.6.1 According to the dictionary, a hot seat is "a precarious, difficult or dangerous situation."

---

* Receiver's Partner is also known as Returner's Partner.

Receiver's Partner | Hot-seat procedure

Following the hot-seat procedure will definitely improve your success in this position.

1. Glance at the service line to see if the serve is long.
2. Focus on Server's Partner to see if she's preparing to poach. Don't watch your partner hit the return.
3. If Server's Partner is about to poach, get ready to defend. Face her head-on, get your center of gravity low, and have your racquet in ready position to use in your defense. If Server's Partner is preparing to hit an overhead, move back farther before she hits.
4. If there's no poach by Server's Partner and the Server isn't serving and volleying, you're out of the hot seat. After the return passes Server's Partner, move forward to your home halfway between the service line and net.
   - If you move too early, you'll risk not being able to defend an attack by Server's Partner.
   - If you move too late, you'll be in the wrong position if the opposing baseline player hits at you.
5. After moving forward, split-step at your home as the baseline player hits the ball.

2.6.2 Watch Server's Partner carefully. The moment the ball goes by her, move quickly forward to your home halfway between the service line and net. If the Server serves and volleys, only move in if your partner hits a low return that will land at the Server's feet. Otherwise, stay where you are on the service line in case the Server hits her first volley at you.

Receiver's Partner | Offensive starting locations

2.6.3 Receiver's Partner might start closer to the net, or move up on the second serve, when Server's Partner never poaches. Note that the Receiver will need to call her own service line.

2.6.4 Starting close to the T is a variation that might disturb the Server. Don't make this your regular starting location as there are also disadvantages. From here, you have farther to go to reach your net player home and you may be in the way of your partner as she returns a T serve.

Receiver's Partner | Defensive starting locations

2.6.5 If Server's Partner is making winners by hitting between you and your partner, start a few steps back, slightly towards the middle. Move forward if Server's Partner doesn't poach the return.

2.6.6 Starting both back can help defend against a strong poacher. It takes the target away from Server's Partner because there's no longer a gap between you and your partner.

Receiver's Partner | Both back as an offensive play

When the Receiver's Partner starts back it's usually because the Server's Partner is poaching well, forcing the Receiving team to defend. However, starting both back can be turned into an offensive play.

Plan this play with your partner before the Server makes her first serve. For example, you might decide to play it for an entire game.

On the first serve, the Receiving team stays back and plays from the defense zone. On a second serve, the Receiver hits deep crosscourt, and both the Receiver and Receiver's Partner charge the net. The Receiver must be sure to keep the crosscourt return out of the reach of Server's Partner.

As Receiver's Partner you have farther to go than your partner. Start running toward the net just before your partner hits the return. (Chapter 4 covers positioning when both partners are up at net.)

This play will only work when the Server's second serve is short enough to approach from (see diagram 4.2.5). However, even if the Receiver ends up unable to approach the net, as Receiver's Partner you can continue running into the net and still get into a good position to play out the point.

2.6.7 Surprise the serving team by having both members of the receiving team charge in.

Receiver's Partner | Key points

The hot-seat procedure teaches where to focus your gaze, how to defend, and when to move forward. Understanding and using it is crucial to your success when playing this position.

Centering Moment
- The usual starting location is on the service line, halfway between the center line and singles sideline.
- Glance at the service line and call balls that land long
- Then watch Server's Partner.

Receiving Phase
- As Receiver's Partner you're in the "hot seat" because of the danger of Server's Partner poaching a weak return and hitting it directly at you.
- If Server's Partner poaches the return, face her, split step, have your racquet in front of your body, and be ready to defend.
- There's almost no backswing on shots hit from the hot seat.

Sending Phase
- If you're successful in reaching a poach by Server's Partner, try not to hit the ball directly back to her. Hit it straight ahead or behind her if possible.
- If Server's Partner doesn't poach, quickly move forward to your home halfway between the net and service line.

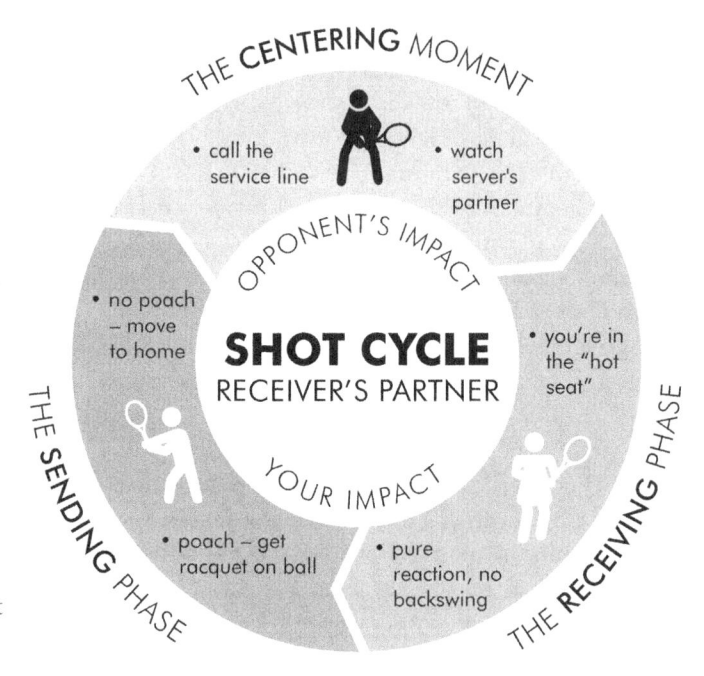

SHOT CYCLE — RECEIVER'S PARTNER

THE CENTERING MOMENT
- call the service line
- watch server's partner

OPPONENT'S IMPACT

THE RECEIVING PHASE
- you're in the "hot seat"
- pure reaction, no backswing

YOUR IMPACT

THE SENDING PHASE
- poach – get racquet on ball
- no poach – move to home

2.7 Serving Team Plays

Serving team plays are planned before the point starts. They add variation and can help your team hold serve. A play is fun to do and it's satisfying when it works.

Confidence with serving and net play, and good communication between partners, are prerequisites for the serving team plays. Higher-level teams can use any of these plays in conjunction with a serve and volley. The following discussion assumes that the Server stays back after the serve.

Of the three serving team plays introduced, Australian formation is emphasized, as it's the easiest play to learn and a good variation for doubles players to know.

Australian formation
- The Server serves from the singles serving position and crosses to other side immediately after her serve.
- Server's Partner starts on the same side as the Server.

I formation
- The Server serves from the singles serving position and moves either left or right.
- Server's Partner starts in front of the Server and moves either left or right to cover the opposite side from the Server.

Planned poach
- The Server and Server's Partner start from the regular positions and switch sides after the serve.

A good doubles team works together. Talk or signal to plan a serving team play before the point begins.

Serving Team Plays | Communication

There are two communication methods you can use to set up plays: talking and signaling. You're only allowed 20 seconds between the end of one point and the start of the next, so you need to be quick. Talking is the simplest method.

- The Server makes the decision about which play to use and where she intends to serve.
- If you have a regular partner, develop your own abbreviations that make your verbal exchange clear and efficient.

With signaling, Server's Partner communicates by using hand signals behind her back. The Server confirms with a verbal "yes" or "no."

- In professional doubles, you'll see Server's Partner signal where the Server should place the serve and which direction Server's Partner will move after the serve.
- For recreational players, the sheer act of using signals may unsettle the receiving team.
- If you want to learn to signal, ask the advice of a coach to ensure both partners understand what to do and where to move.

2.7.1 If you talk between points, Server's Partner should move back to meet the Server. This conserves Server's energy and gives her more time to mentally prepare for the serve.

Serving Team Plays | Australian formation

Australian formation is a versatile play that puts pressure on the receiving team. It's named after the Australian professional players who first used it.

This formation is successfully used by recreational players from the NTRP 3.0 level and up. You can play it on as few or many points as you like.

The Set-up

The Server starts from the singles serving location close to the center mark.

- Immediately after serving, the Server moves laterally to cover the other side.
- The Server is responsible for down-the-line shots and crosscourt lobs.

The Server's Partner starts on the same side as the Server near the center line, a step farther back than usual.

- The Server's Partner is responsible for crosscourt and down-the-middle returns, including crosscourt lobs that aren't too deep.
- The Server's Partner should take any ball she can reach, even if it means crossing over to the other side.

If the Receiver hits her return down the line, the point will continue in a Playing Straight formation (see section 3.5).

2.7.2 When first learning Australian, play practice matches where both teams use it on every point. This will get you familiar with both the serving and receiving roles.

Serving Team Plays | Server's partner in Australian formation

2.7.3 As Server's Partner, your starting location is close to the center line. From here, you must stay alert and be ready to move diagonally forward in either direction.

2.7.4 When playing Australian, don't start in the usual Server's Partner location. This leaves the majority of the court for your partner to cover and opens up a hole (white area) after she crosses to the other side.

Serving Team Plays | How to use Australian

Practice Australian with your partner before using it in a match. Talk briefly or use signals to decide to play Australian and then move to your new starting locations.

When to use Australian:
- early in the match to test out its effectiveness against your opponents;
- the Receiver is making winning crosscourt returns as it will force her to hit down the line to avoid Server's Partner;
- your serve is regularly being broken;
- you're a singles player who serves much better from the singles serving position.

Keep your serves deep, and mix up hitting in different directions. Notice which serves work best and use them most of the time. Before each serve, remind yourself which way you'll need to move after the serve.

Use Australian occasionally, so the receiving team has to keep adjusting, or use it most or all of the time if it's working well. You can also play Australian only on the first serve, moving back to a regular starting position on the second.

Don't be discouraged and give up playing Australian if you lose a point or two. As long as you break even, winning at least half of the Australian points you attempt, it's worth using.

2.7.5 Play Australian on both serves or just the first. To use only on the first, simply move to the regular starting positions for the second serve.

Serving Team Plays | Ad-court Australian

Ad-court Australian (Server serves from the ad side) is the most common play for a number of reasons.
- It's easier for the right-handed Server to avoid her partner on the serve. There's no need for Server's Partner to crouch or kneel down.
- After the Server moves right, she can use her forehand to drive the ball deep to the Receiver's backhand.
- The Server's Partner's forehand volley is on the inside, which puts her in a strong position to poach.

When to use ad-court Australian:
- the Receiver is making winning crosscourt backhand returns as, to avoid Server's Partner, she'll have to hit her backhand down the line;
- a left-handed Receiver is making strong crosscourt returns with her forehand and the Server is having difficulty placing the serve down the T to her backhand;
- you're struggling to win points serving from and playing on the ad side;
- the score is ad-in on a long service game. This simple act of changing the starting arrangement often draws an error from the Receiver;
- during a tie-break if ad-court Australian has been working for you so far.

2.7.6 Ad-court Australian is a perfect play if the Server prefers to play points from the deuce side and has a strong down-the-line forehand.

Serving Team Plays | Deuce-court Australian

Deuce-court Australian (Server serves from the deuce side) is used less often than its ad court counterpart.
- It's more difficult for a right-handed Server to avoid Server's Partner on the serve.
- After the Server has moved to the left she'll have her backhand on the outside. The net player has her backhand in the middle.

Even so, it can work well when used at the right time. It's especially effective if one of the partners is left-handed.

When to use deuce-court Australian:
- the Receiver is clearly unfamiliar with the Australian formation and is struggling with the return;
- the Receiver is making winning forehand crosscourt returns as, to avoid Server's Partner, she'll have to hit her forehand down the line;
- you're having trouble getting the serve to the backhand side of the Receiver;
- you're a left-handed Server. It's easier avoid your partner on the serve and your forehand will be on the outside after you move to the left;
- you're a left-handed Server's Partner with a strong forehand poach as it puts your forehand in the middle.

2.7.7 Server's Partner may need to crouch down or start farther over toward the sideline to avoid being in the way of the serve.

Serving Team Plays | Responding to lobs when playing Australian

2.7.8 As Server, you're responsible for covering crosscourt lobs. You need to readjust your direction of movement when you see the Receiver's lob. Alert your partner to switch to the other side.

2.7.9 A deep crosscourt lob neutralizes the effectiveness of Australian and may be challenging for you, as the Server, to return with your backhand. If the Receiver is making effective crosscourt lob returns, Server's Partner can discourage the lob by starting on the service line.

Serving Team Plays | Receiving team's response to Australian formation

When you see your opponents setting up for Australian, adjust your starting locations.

- The Receiver moves a step toward the center mark to place herself in the middle of the new possible angles of the serve.
- Receiver's Partner moves a couple of steps closer to the center line. Follow the usual hot-seat procedure and move in after the return has passed Server's Partner.

Receiver, take a deep breath, relax and think "down the line."

- To avoid the net player, your best option is a down-the-line return.
- On a short serve you can return down the line and approach the net (see diagram 4.2.11).
- A crosscourt lob return is another option if you can reliably hit this shot.
- The crosscourt lob will be more effective when returning from the ad side as it will land on the backhand side of the baseline player.

As Receiver, be aware that the Server is in a better position to hit to the T. Remind yourself to be ready for the T serve. You may not see it coming because Server's Partner tends to obscure your view of the Server.

2.7.10 When faced with Australian, plan where you want to hit the return before the serve. Stick with your plan to avoid getting distracted by any movements of Server's Partner

Serving Team Plays | Australian variation

You can start in Australian formation and move into a regular one-up and one-back formation after the serve. Use this variation to create uncertainty for the receiving team if you're playing a lot of points using Australian. Or use it playing from the deuce side to make it easier to place your serve down the T without having to end up in a playing-straight formation (see section 3.5).

The Server starts close to the center mark and moves laterally toward the same-side sideline. Server's Partner starts in the Australian starting location and moves quickly to cover the opposite side as soon as the serve crosses the net.

You'll need to have regular communication with your partner to set this up without forewarning your opponents of the change-up. One option is for Server's Partner to signal "stay" or "go" on every Australian point. Make sure you're both clear about which direction to move.

- The signal for "stay" is a closed fist behind Server's Partner's back. It means that Server's Partner will stay on the same side where she began.
- The signal for "go" is an open hand. In Australian variation, the Server's Partner goes and crosses to the other side.

2.7.11 The Australian variation is shown on the ad side. The variation can also be played with deuce-court Australian. To avoid confusion, before you hit your serve, remind yourself which direction you'll need to move after you serve.

Serving Team Plays | Australian both back

Australian both back is a little known formation that may lead to an error by the Receiver simply because it looks so unusual. It can be played with the Server starting from the deuce or ad side.

The Server serves from the singles serving position and moves laterally to cover the other side immediately after serving. Server's Partner starts on the baseline near the singles sideline, on the same side as the Server.

When to use Australian both back:
- Server's Partner is struggling at the net;
- Server's Partner prefers the baseline. The Server will be able to get into net after the point starts;
- because it's fun and different.

Receiver's Response
As Receiver you have the freedom to hit the ball anywhere. Decide where you'll hit a forehand or backhand return before the serve and watch the ball as you hit.
- A solid down-the-middle return may cause confusion for the serving team.
- Hit to the weaker player's weaker side.
- Use a drop-shot return if you have this shot in your repertoire.

2.7.12 The serving team must watch out for the down-the-middle return. Decide in advance who will take this ball.

Serving Team Plays | I formation (original)

The I formation is a serving team play that provides Server's Partner with good poaching opportunities. It gets it name from the way the players line up one in front of the other, like the two ends of the capital letter **I**.

The I formation creates uncertainty for the receiving team as they don't know which way the serving team will move. I formation can be equally effective played from the deuce or ad side.

Both serving team players line up one behind the other.
- The Server serves from close to the center mark.
- Server's Partner crouches low or kneels on one knee, straddling the center line.
- Before the serve, partners agree which side they'll each cover after the serve.

This formation puts pressure on the Receiver because she doesn't know which way the serving team will be moving and the net player seems to be on top of the net, ready to poach the ball no matter which way she returns.

The Receiver's go-to return is down the line, as Server's Partner has farther to travel to cover this direction. A crosscourt lob return is another good option.

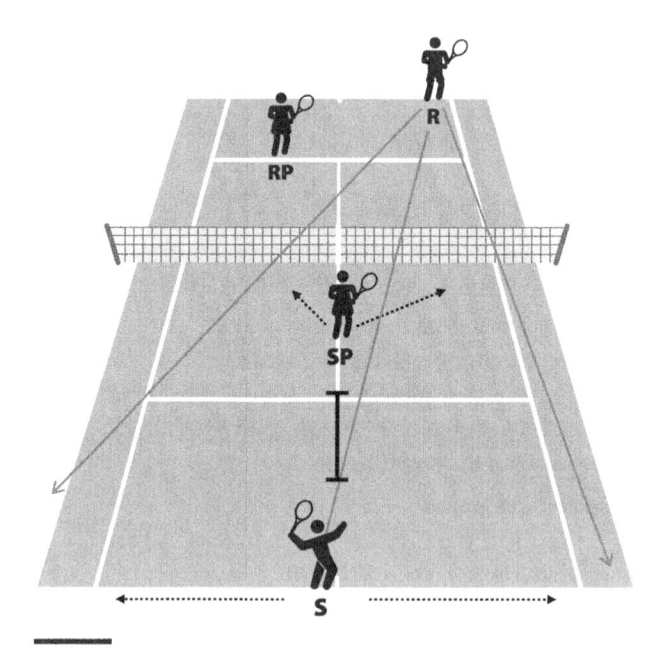

2.7.13 Notice how Server's Partner has farther to go to reach a down-the-line return compared to a crosscourt return.

Serving Team Plays | I formation (modern)

In the modern I formation, the Server's Partner starts on the opposite side of the Server, close to the center line. This positioning puts Server's Partner in the exact middle of the possible angles the Receiver can hit.

Server's Partner can move with equal ease to either the left or right. This provides an advantage over the original I formation as it's even more difficult for the Receiver to predict which way Server's Partner will move and there's no obvious space to hit the return into.

In both variations, however, the Server and Server's Partner move to their new locations before the Receiver hits the ball. If the Receiver is versatile, she can adjust the placement of her return after the Server's Partner moves.

The I formation can be successfully used by recreational players from about the NTRP 3.5 level up. A thorough understanding and execution of the concepts and tactics in this book is a prerequisite. When you're ready, a coach can teach you the details of the I formation.

Some drawbacks of the I formation include the amount of time it takes to learn, the need for a regular partner to play it well, and the physical demands of the Server's Partner's crouching position.

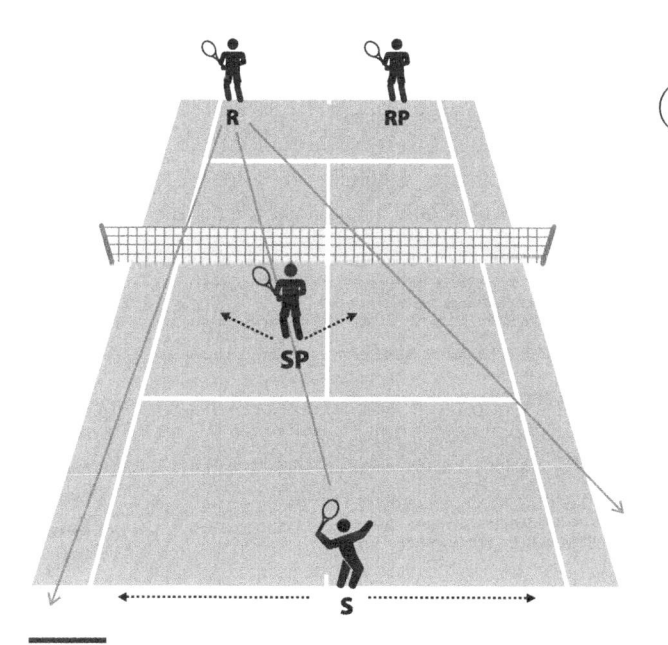

2.7.14 If you watch professional doubles matches, you'll regularly see the players using the modern version of the I formation. Receiver's Partner often starts at the baseline because Server's Partner's poaches are so effective.

Serving Team Plays | Planned poach

The planned poach is an agreed switch that's arranged in advance by the serving team with the hope that Server's Partner can poach the return.

Both Server and Server's Partner start in their usual starting locations and switch sides after the serve. The Server moves laterally to the other side immediately after serving.

- As Server, you're responsible for down-the-line shots and lobs that go over your partner.
- There's a farther distance to travel than in Australian so you must move to the other side quickly.

As the ball lands in the service box, Server's Partner moves to just past the center line, faces the Receiver and split steps when the return is hit.

- After the split step, Server's Partner must be ready to move diagonally forward in either direction.
- As Server's Partner, you're responsible for the middle ball and all crosscourt drives.
- This move is called an "early leave," as the Receiver will see you start to cross to the other side before she hits her return.
- You're committed to covering the other side, even if the Receiver hits a wide-angled crosscourt.

2.7.15 A planned poach serving from the deuce side provides an opportunity for you, as Server's Partner, to poach on your forehand side. Regardless of whether or not you intercept the return, recover to your home on the deuce side (see diagram 3.5.6).

Serving Team Plays | How to use the planned poach

The success of the planned poach depends on surprising the receiving team. Practice the planned poach with your partner before trying it out in a match so you can execute it smoothly.

Talk briefly with your partner or use signals to decide to use a planned poach. It's best if your partner knows ahead where you intend to place the serve. You need to be already routinely communicating between points so the receiving team does not suspect your plan.

The planned poach works best on a strong first serve, especially one with power. Angled, T or body serves can all work for this play. As you become more adept with the planned poach, Server's Partner should learn to adjust the location of her split step depending on where the serve lands (see diagrams 2.7.17 and 2.7.18).

When to use a planned poach:
- the Server has an unusually powerful serve;
- Server's Partner is especially quick and confident playing at net;
- early in the match to test out its effectiveness against your opponents;
- the Receiver is making winning crosscourt returns;
- if you're losing against a stronger team, try it out. You have nothing to lose.

2.7.16 A planned poach serving from the ad side may be more difficult for a right-handed Server's Partner, as you're poaching from your backhand side as you switch across to poach the return. If you're a lefty, however, you'll be poaching with your forehand as you switch across.

Serving Team Plays | Adjustments when using the planned poach

2.7.17 With a planned poach, the exact spot where the Server's Partner should split step changes according to different serve placements. On an angled serve, your split step is on the center line.

2.7.18 On a T serve, Server's Partner must move farther, a couple of steps across the center line, to be properly centered in relation to the new possible angles of the return of serve.

Serving Team Plays | Receiving team's response to the planned poach

The planned poach is designed to come as a surprise to the receiving team. Rest assured that as Receiver, you'll see your opponents moving before you hit your return. When you see them move, you'll probably want to change your plan about where to return the ball.

Once you have seen them move and made a new plan about where to hit, stop watching your opponents and watch the ball.

Return options:
- Down the line is the most common return;
- A defensive crosscourt lob is a good option if the serve is powerful.

There are other creative return options if you're not getting rattled by your opponent's movements:
- short-angle crosscourt;
- down the middle.

Receiver's Partner must stay alert and be ready to defend if Server's Partner intercepts the return. Once the ball passes Server's Partner, Receiver's Partner moves forward and looks for a possible poach.

If your opponents have played a successful planned poach, shake it off without letting it affect your regular crosscourt return. Remember that the most important thing you can do as the Receiver is to be calm and ready for anything, split stepping as the Server strikes the ball.

2.7.19 When faced with the planned poach, down the line is your go-to return, or, if the serve is powerful, try a defensive lob.

Starting the Point | Summary

How you begin each point has an enormous effect on the outcome of the match. Understanding your responsibilities and proper starting location for each of the four starting positions, and knowing how and when to change your location, will definitely improve your game.

Server
- The most important thing is to get the point started, ideally getting in at least 75 percent of your first serves.
- Once you can get the ball in, develop your serve by learning to hit with depth, direction, spin and increased power.

Server's Partner
- Be active at net, while leaving difficult balls traveling down the middle and deeper lobs for your partner.
- If you're feeling overpowered by the return of serve, move back to the baseline.
- Learning to fake can be remarkably effective against a Receiver who likes to hit down the alley.

Receiver
- The most important thing is to get the return in play, ideally keeping it away from Server's Partner.
- Hit about 80 percent of your returns crosscourt.
- Take the time to develop specialty shots that work reliably when faced with an active Server's Partner.
- Consider specializing on the deuce or ad side, weighing your strengths, weaknesses and personality in your decision.

Receiver's Partner
- Watch Server's Partner and be ready to defend against a poach if your partner hits a weak return.
- Learn the correct procedure for moving from the starting location on the service line into the net after the ball has passed Server's Partner.

Serving Team Plays
- Learn how to play Australian and how to respond to a team playing the Australian formation.
- Experiment with the planned poach, especially if your team includes a strong Server and agile net player.

CHAPTER 3

One Up and One Back

3.1 One-Up and One-Back Formation

After the point has started, each doubles team moves into a playing formation. The most common way to play the point at all levels of play is both teams playing one up and one back. Developing a strong one-up and one-back game is good preparation for learning other formations.

In one up and one back, one partner plays close to the net (up), while the other plays from the baseline (back).

The baseline player plays from a home in the defense zone and hits shots to set up his partner at net. The net player's home is in the offense zone and puts the ball away. Typically the baseline player hits crosscourt until the net player can cut off a crosscourt ball with a poach.

Advantages
- It's easy get into as most points start in this arrangement.
- It's clear who takes the lobs. The baseline player covers all deep lobs.

Big Disadvantage
- It leaves a gap between partners where the opposing net player can hit a winning volley.

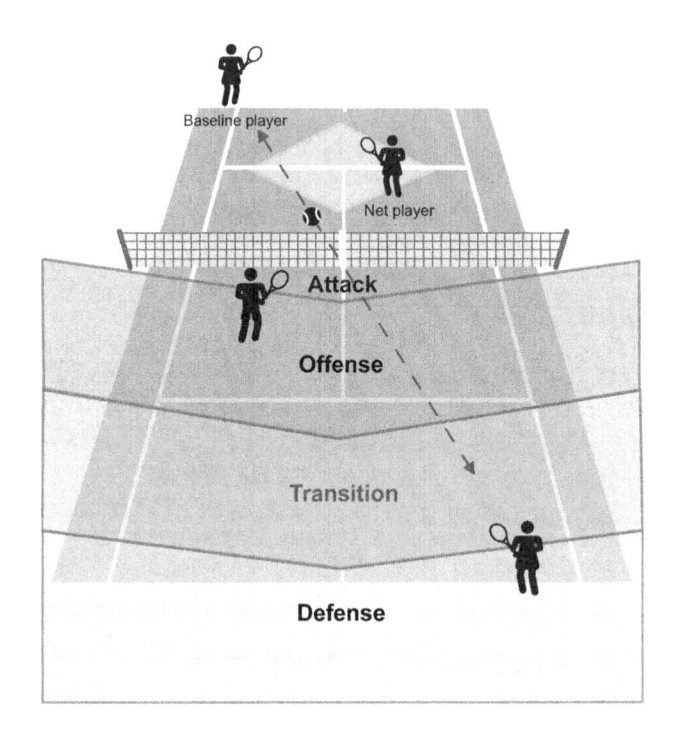

3.1.1 Here both teams are playing one up and one back. Notice the gap between the baseline player and net player, marked by the white diamond in the far end of the court.

One-Up and One-Back Formation | Target areas

The place where you aim to hit your ball is called a target area. In a system developed by Helle Sparre (2004), the court is divided into five target areas that include four triangles and one diamond.

The baseline player's primary target is to hit into the deep-crosscourt triangle.

- This is sometimes described as hitting "deep to deep." The player who is deep in the court (baseline player) hits the ball back deep in the court.

The net player's primary target is to hit between the two opponents, into the diamond in the center.

- This is sometimes described as hitting "short to short." The player in the short part of the court (net player) hits the ball back in the front (or short) part of the court.
- Players are often taught to hit at the opposite net player's feet, which is also a "short to short" tactic. This may work at the lower levels, but experienced net players develop good reflexes and can return these balls.

The diamond and triangle targets areas will be referred to throughout the remainder of this book.

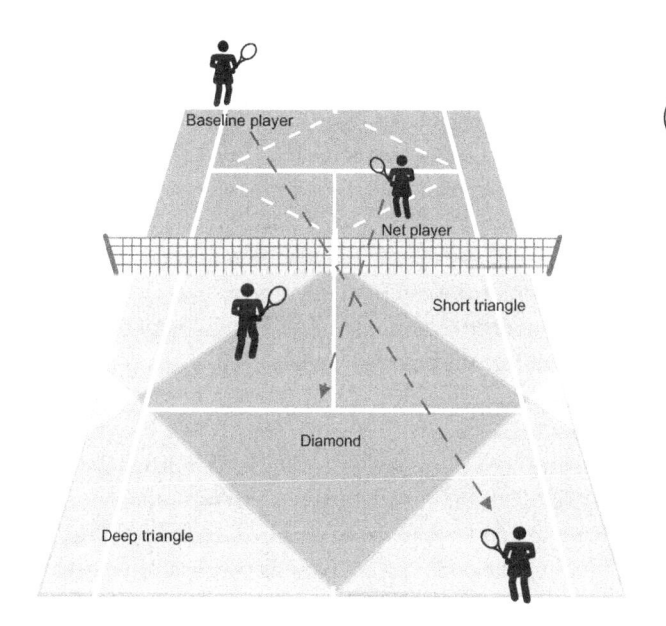

3.1.2 Create target areas during practice by placing line markers to make up the four sides of the diamond as shown on the far end of the court. This creates both the diamond and the four triangles.

3.2 The Net Player

Once the point is under way, the roles of Server's Partner and Receiver's Partner dissolve as these two players both become net players.

The net player's primary job is to finish the point by hitting into the diamond-shaped gap between the two opponents.

The net player's home is in the offense zone, at approximately the center of the service box. This is where you need to be centered and ready every time your opponent hits the ball. More advanced players constantly adjust the exact location of their home, depending on where the ball is in the opposing court.

As the net player, you're responsible for drives down the alley, balls hit directly at you, short lobs, shots down the middle that can be poached, and, if possible, defending the opposing net player's poaches. Hit any ball that you can comfortably reach. You also need to learn when to leave difficult balls that are more easily taken by your partner at the baseline.

Occasionally you'll run to the other side of the court to retrieve a short ball that would be difficult for your partner to reach (see diagram 3.3.12). Lobs that go over you are covered by your partner at the baseline.

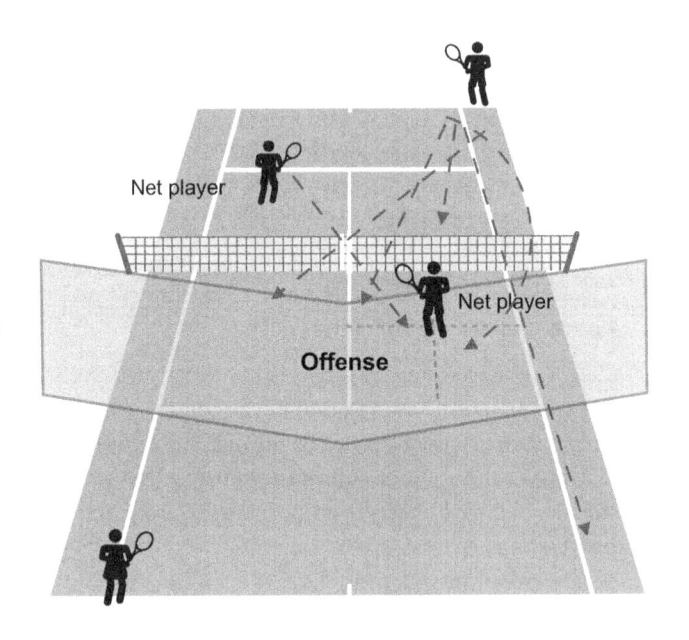

3.2.1 As the net player, remain patient and alert, even when you're not hitting any balls. Staying calm and keeping your feet moving throughout the entire point will help you avoid the trap of becoming over-excited when you finally get to hit a ball.

The Net Player | Play from the correct home

The net player's home is at the center of the service box. Within two steps of this location you can cover more than half of the court, so long as the ball you're receiving is a drive and not a lob. This position slightly favors covering the middle of the court over covering the alley. It's okay to tempt the opposing baseline player to hit down the alley as this is a lower percentage shot and may result in an error.

The most common positional error is to play from a home too far back. Some players start in the correct position but drift back as the point progresses. Hold your ground.

From the correct home:
- You can move forward into the attack zone to put the ball away.
- You can cover more area than from farther back.
- It's easier to deflect a hard hit ball and get it over the net.

Standing too close to the net is also not advised. If you're too close to the net there's no room to move forward on a poach and even a short lob will go over you. However, there's one exception. If you find that the opposing baseline player is regularly lobbing just out of your reach, make your home farther back so you can get into the action.

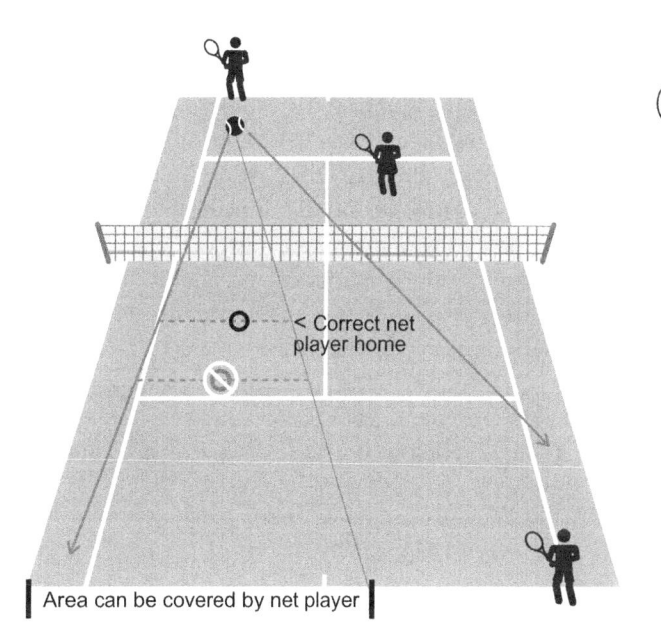

| Area can be covered by net player |

3.2.2 The distance to cover the same court area increases as you move back from the correct home. Having more area to cover is a big liability because you only have time to take one or two steps before you hit your volley.

The Net Player | How to poach

To "poach" is to intercept a ball that the opposing baseline player has intended for your partner at the baseline. Poaching is not really stealing, as the name might imply. It's the net player's legal job!

Learn to poach at the right opportunity, without hitting inappropriate or out balls, lunging for a ball you don't hit, or getting in the way of your partner. Avoid taking a swing at the ball unless you can hit it. If you swing without making contact, it's very difficult for your partner to adjust to cover the ball.

You can anticipate when to poach by watching your opponent's movement, body position, and racquet as he prepares to hit the ball. If he's off balance or stretching to reach the ball, you may be able to poach.

To poach, move a step toward the middle as your opponent starts his forward swing. Most of the time you won't actually intercept the ball but the movement itself puts pressure on the opposing baseline player. If you can reach the ball, take a diagonal step forward into the attack zone to hit your volley.

Sometimes you'll end up crossing into the other service box to hit your poach. In this case, stay on the new side and let your partner cross behind you.

3.2.3 Hitting from inside the attack zone is the key to great poaching. From here your racquet is higher than the net when you make contact which allows you to hit down on the ball. You're go-to target is into the open space between the two opponents. Whether or not you hit the poach, immediately move back to your home in the offense zone.

The Net Player | To poach or not to poach

Find a balance between being active at net and waiting for the correct ball to poach. Low or difficult balls traveling down the middle are best left for the baseline player. If you have to move backward to intercept a ball, let it go through to your partner.

Be especially discerning when poaching from the deuce side as a right-hander. A ball traveling past your backhand side could be an easy shot for your partner's forehand groundstroke.

If you're left-handed, make extra effort to develop your poach from the deuce side. The extra reach your forehand provides will surprise the opposing baseline player over and over again.

As net player, be more conservative about the balls you try to poach if you're regularly making errors on your poaches.

However, don't make erratic or dramatic changes. Be consistent about how far you move to poach balls. Your partner depends on you to regularly cover the same general area. Note that it's appropriate for your general area to be different when playing from the deuce versus the ad side.

3.2.4 You're in a weak position to poach when you're reaching for a ball from far back in the service box. Let the ball go through to your partner's forehand.

The Net Player | Cover the alley on an outside ball

As the net player, you're responsible for covering drives hit down your alley. On an outside ball that's pulling your opponent outside of her doubles sideline, move to a home closer to the singles sideline.
- Angle your body so you're facing the ball.
- Be ready to move diagonally forward in either direction.
- Never stand in the alley or on the singles sideline. This leaves too much area for your partner to cover.

Make your opponent prove he can successfully hit the down-the-alley shot from the outside ball more than once or twice. If he's missing one for every one he makes, you're better off focusing your attention on poaching the crosscourt balls.

If your opponent is regularly winning points hitting down the alley on an outside ball, make some changes.
- Notice when he likes to hit down the alley and pay attention when that situation arises.
- Use the fake (see diagram 2.4.6) to bait him into hitting down the alley, then move to cover his shot.
- Have your partner avoid hitting the wide-angle shot that sets your opponent up to hit down the alley.

3.2.5 Don't overreact if the occasional shot goes down your alley, even if your opponents are celebrating. Being obsessed with covering the alley paralyzes your ability to do the more important job of poaching balls traveling down the middle.

The Net Player | Cover the alley on an inside ball

The opposing baseline player can also hit down the alley from the inside of the court. In general, a down-the-line shot hit from an inside ball is easier to control than one hit from an outside ball. For right-handers, the inside shot uses a backhand on the deuce side and forehand on the ad side.

It's easy to forget that your opponent may hit down your alley on an inside ball when you're focusing on poaching. Be mentally prepared to protect your alley any time during a point, especially when your opponent is well set up and hitting an inside ball on his forehand side. Note that a left-handed player playing on the deuce side has his forehand on the inside and will likely have this shot perfected.

Even if you're actively looking for and moving to poach, don't drift toward the middle of your court as the point progresses. Be centered at your home every time your opponent hits the ball.

Pay attention to your opponents' tendencies over the course of a match to learn which balls they regularly hit down the alley. Be aware that within a point, the baseline player will probably use the same specialty shots he likes to hit on his service returns.

3.2.6 Focusing exclusively on poaching makes you vulnerable to a passing shot down your alley from an inside ball.

The Net Player | Targets

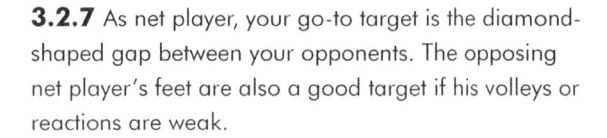

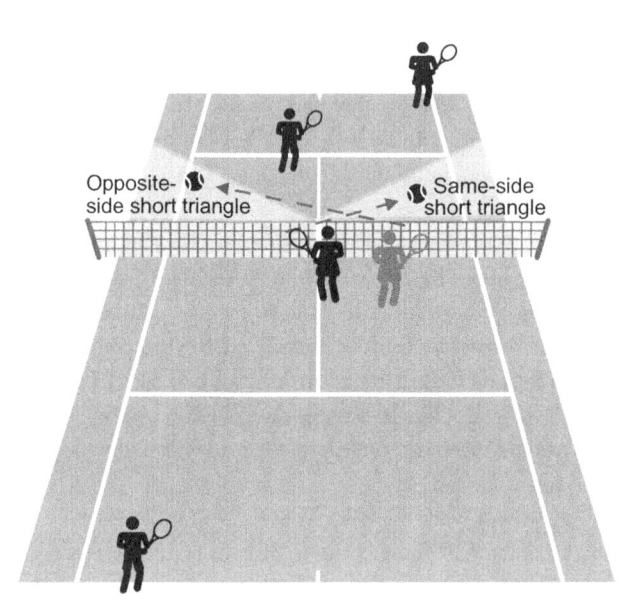

3.2.7 As net player, your go-to target is the diamond-shaped gap between your opponents. The opposing net player's feet are also a good target if his volleys or reactions are weak.

3.2.8 Advanced targets include the opposite-side short triangle (when the opposing net player is covering the middle), and the same-side short triangle (when moving across the court for a poach). Only hit to the same-side short triangle when you're sure you can hit a winner. If you hit this shot too deep, it leaves plenty of open court for the opposing baseline player.

The Net Player | Get out of trouble

3.2.9 A powerful or difficult ball coming toward you that clearly belongs to you should be deflected back toward the baseline player as deep as possible. If you try to hit these types of balls into the diamond, you're likely to set up the opposing net player.

3.2.10 After making a poor poach, get back to your home quickly to help salvage the point. Expect the net player to aim for the space you've opened up behind you.

The Net Player | Play defense in offense

A great net player always seems to be in the right place at the right time. To become one of these players, learn to move back and forward during the point. I call this the defense-in-offense method.

If the ball is behind you, you're on defense. Move back and toward the center line.

- Usually you have enough time to move back two or three steps.
- Watch the diagonal net player and be ready to defend if he poaches.

If the ball is in front of you, you're on offense. Move forward to your home.

- Move forward to your home as soon as the ball has passed the opposite net player.
- If you can't make it all the way to your home in time, don't move so far back in the first place.
- Get centered and ready as the baseline player hits the ball.
- Be alert for poaching opportunities, moving diagonally forward if you suspect you can intercept the baseline player's crosscourt ball.

If you're tired, forgo using this movement pattern. If your mobility is limited, only move back a little.

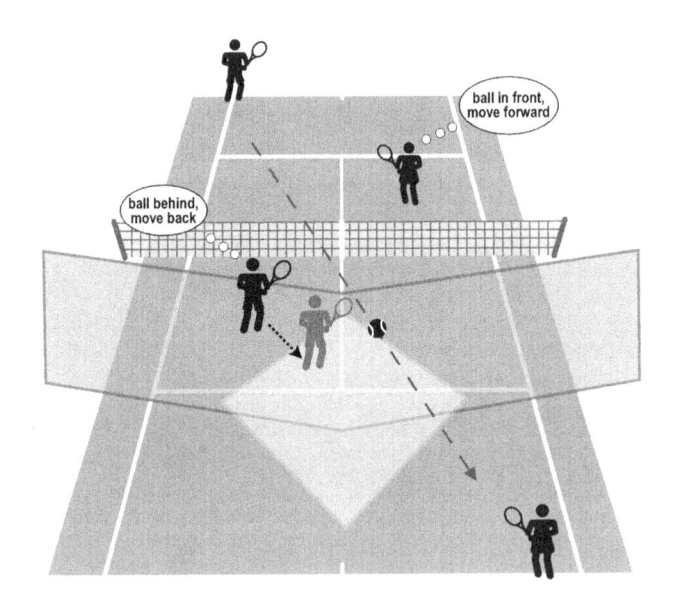

3.2.11 This movement pattern should only be attempted when you're very comfortable playing from the correct net player home. Bottom line: Be centered and ready at your home in the center of the service box by the time the baseline player hits the ball.

The Net Player | Gaze points

The ability to be at the right place at the right time is further enhanced by focusing your gaze and attention at the correct place. This is similar to the skill that Receiver's Partner uses in the hot-seat procedure (see diagram 2.6.2).

When the ball is behind you:
- Watch the diagonal net player's movement and racquet.
- You'll immediately see if he plans to poach and you'll be ready to defend sooner.
- Listen for the sound of your partner moving and hitting instead of watching him.

Don't look behind at your partner.
- You lose the valuable time and early warning you need to prepare for an attack by the opposing net player.
- If you must look behind to help with a line call, make it a quick glance. Then immediately focus your gaze on the net player.

When the ball is in front of you and has passed the net player:
- Watch the ball.
- Notice where both opponents are positioned.
- Watch the movement and racquet of the baseline player hitting the ball.

3.2.12 If you habitually turn back to watch your partner, in the beginning you'll need to be disciplined and not look back at all. It may feel very strange or scary. Soon you'll discover the advantage of focusing your attention at the opposing net player rather than looking back.

The Net Player | Defend against a poach or overhead

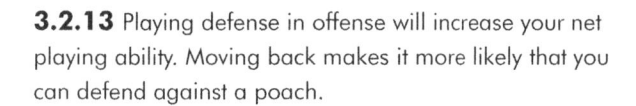

3.2.13 Playing defense in offense will increase your net playing ability. Moving back makes it more likely that you can defend against a poach.

3.2.14 When your partner hits a short lob you have time to move even farther back. Scoot back until just before the opposing net player strikes the ball, then split step and get ready to pick up anything you can reach.

The Net Player | Move forward when the ball is in front

3.2.15 When the ball in the far court is out wide, move forward and center yourself closer to the sideline. Be mentally and physically ready to cover the alley or move to intercept a crosscourt ball.

3.2.16 When the ball in the far court is closer to the middle, move to the usual home in the center of the service box. Remain alert to the possibility that the opposing baseline player could hit the inside ball down your alley.

The Net Player | Triangular movement pattern

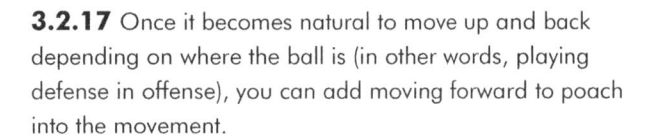

3.2.17 Once it becomes natural to move up and back depending on where the ball is (in other words, playing defense in offense), you can add moving forward to poach into the movement.

3.2.18 If you're not successful at cutting off a poach, move straight back to your defense position when the ball is behind you. You're now moving in a triangular pattern.

The Net Player | Develop a "good eye"

A player is said to have a "good eye" if he can consistently sense when not to hit a ball that's in his hitting range but is going to land out. A good eye takes time and awareness to develop. Fortunately there are things you can do to accelerate the process.

- Be aware that as the net player, you have a responsibility to leave balls that are going out.
- When practicing or warming up, don't volley balls you think will go out, either wide or long.
- Sometimes you'll have to dodge a ball hit hard at you that's going out.
- When playing points, have the courage not to hit balls you sense are going out. If you occasionally leave a ball that lands in, don't give up.
- If you're playing socially with good friends, ask their opinion whether they think a ball you hit would have gone out. The player who hit the ball to you is usually the best judge of whether it would have been in or out.

Occasionally your partner at the baseline will have time and be in a good position to verbally warn you if a ball is going out.

3.2.19 Most recreational players, especially those new to the game, find it difficult to judge whether a ball will be in or out. A good eye can be developed just like any other skill.

The Net Player | Key points

Centering Moment
- Be in the best possible position to either attack or defend as your opponent hits the ball.
- Center yourself every time the opponent hits the ball, even if you don't think it will be you who hits the ball.
- Remain patient and calm for the entire point.

Receiving Phase
- The receiving phase is usually very short if you're hitting a volley. Get turned before the ball coming toward you crosses the net.
- Sometimes you have to use your perception skills to decide not to hit a ball that's in your hitting range but will land out.
- Once the ball has gone by you, your team is still in the receiving phase as your partner prepares to hit. Move back slightly and get ready to defend in case your partner's shot gets poached by the opposing net player.

Sending Phase
- The center of the diamond, between your two opponents, is your go-to target for poaches.
- Most volleys have little follow-through.
- After hitting, recover quickly to your correct home (or as close as you can get to it) before your opponent strikes the ball.

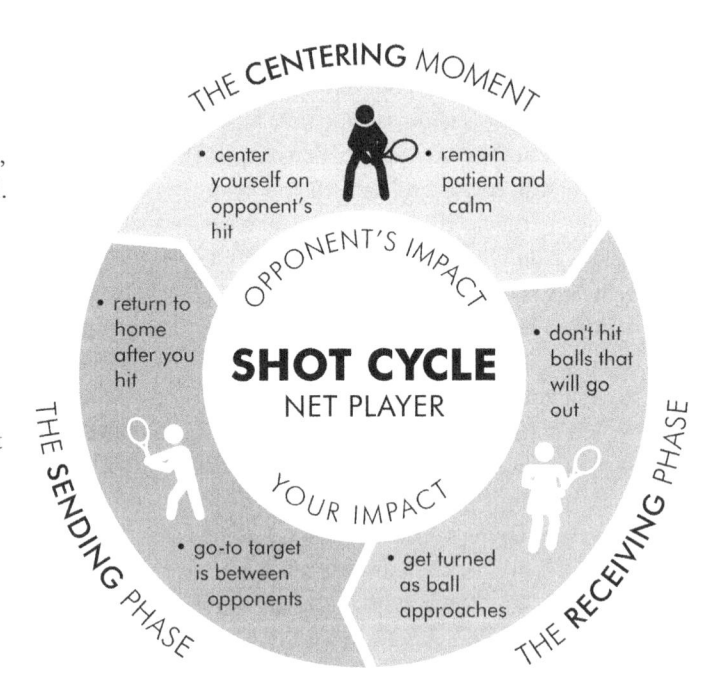

SHOT CYCLE — NET PLAYER

THE CENTERING MOMENT
- center yourself on opponent's hit
- remain patient and calm

OPPONENT'S IMPACT

THE RECEIVING PHASE
- don't hit balls that will go out
- get turned as ball approaches

YOUR IMPACT

THE SENDING PHASE
- go-to target is between opponents
- return to home after you hit

3.3 The Baseline Player

Once the point is under way, the roles of Server and Receiver dissolve as both of these players become baseline players.

As the baseline player, you have three different strategies available to help your team win points:
1. Win the point from the baseline.
2. Hit shots that set up the net player to hit a winning volley
3. Approach the net to move into a both-up formation (covered in Chapter 4).

The baseline player's home is just behind the baseline near the singles sideline. More experienced players continually fine tune the exact position of their home, depending on the location and difficulty of the ball in the opposing court.

As the baseline player, you're responsible for covering crosscourt drives and lobs, middle balls your partner doesn't hit, and down-the-line lobs over your partner. In addition, try and reach any ball that gets by your partner.

If possible, verbally warn the net player if you think a ball he might hit will go out. "Bounce It" or "no" are examples of appropriate warnings. "Out" is not acceptable as this call is reserved for the line call after a ball has landed.

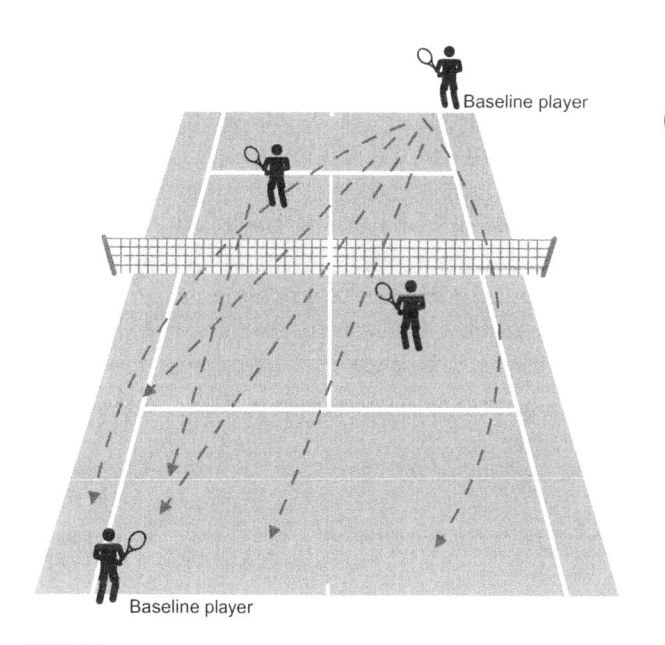

3.3.1 When playing from the baseline, you must cover a wide variety of shots from your home in the defense zone. You have much more time to reach balls than your partner playing at the net because you're farther back and the balls bounce.

The Baseline Player | Play from the correct home

As a baseline player, your most important positional skill is to recover to your correct home after every hit. From the baseline home you can move in any direction to receive a ball: left, right, forward, back, or diagonal.

The baseline player's home is in the defense zone, behind the baseline and near the singles sideline. If you play a lot of singles, you'll need to train yourself not to move toward the middle after you hit.

Two common baseline player errors are playing from a home inside the baseline or creeping into the transition zone as the point progresses, and playing too close to the middle of the court.

The exact home position varies somewhat, depending on:
- your personal preferences;
- whether you're right- or left-handed;
- your opponents' tendencies;
- where the ball is on the other side of the court;
- the difficulty of the ball on the other side of the court.

When playing from the correct home located behind the baseline, always let the ball bounce. It's shocking how many baseline players habitually give away points by hitting balls that would have gone out.

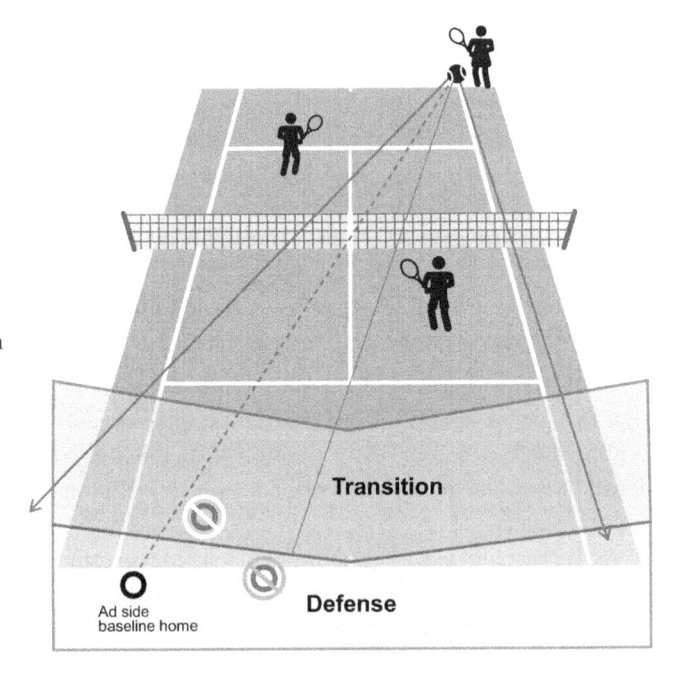

3.3.2 When you examine the angles available to the opposing baseline player, it becomes apparent why the baseline home is close to the singles sideline.

The Baseline Player | Win from the baseline

The first and most basic baseline player strategy is to win the point from the baseline.

Hitting crosscourt with patience and consistency will often win the point, especially at lower levels of play. In fact, the ability to hit crosscourt consistently while avoiding the net player is a fundamental doubles skill.

There are different tactics you can use to win from the baseline. Always consider how best to use your strengths to attack your opponents' weaknesses.

- Out-steady or over-power the baseline player while keeping the ball out of reach of the net player.
- Hit to the weaker side of the baseline player.
- Move the baseline player side-to-side by hitting one ball deep and wide, and the next low and down the middle.
- Hit short and wide if the baseline player does not move forward well.
- Hit a short ball to intentionally draw a player who prefers to play the baseline into the net. Then lob over or hit directly at him.
- When you want or need to hit near the net player, hit either low or high to keep it out of his strike zone (chest height) or hit with power directly at him.

3.3.3 It's easier to hit a short-angled shot from a ball that lands in your alley. Beware, you may get a return that's even more angled.

The Baseline Player | Change the direction

As a point progresses, you may be able to win the point from the baseline by changing from a crosscourt to a down-the-line direction. The specialty shots you have developed on your return of serve (see diagrams 2.5.8 and 2.5.9) can now be used within the point.

- Lob over the net player.
- Hit with power directly at the net player.
- Hit down the alley from either the outside or inside ball. Use this shot only when you're relaxed, well balanced, and the opposing net player appears to be leaving the alley unguarded.

Many recreational players hit down-the-line shots too often and too soon in the point. Don't change the direction because you don't know what else to do. You'll have the most success hitting down the line if you wait until the opposing net player is out of position or has become disengaged.

Notice if you tend to change the direction to try and win quickly on important points, such as game points or during a tiebreak. This is the time to relax, play your most patient tennis, and wait for the right opportunity to finish the point.

3.3.4 The lob over the net player is most effective when the ball lands on the opposite baseline player's backhand side. Use this shot after you have pulled the opposite baseline player out wide or if he has difficulty hitting high backhands.

The Baseline Player | Hit down the alley

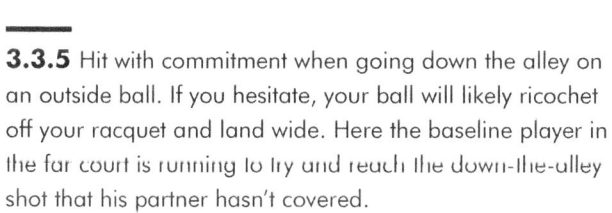

3.3.5 Hit with commitment when going down the alley on an outside ball. If you hesitate, your ball will likely ricochet off your racquet and land wide. Here the baseline player in the far court is running to try and reach the down-the-alley shot that his partner hasn't covered.

3.3.6 It's easier to control the down-the-alley shot on an inside ball. Wait until the right opportunity to hit this shot by keeping the rally going crosscourt until the net player becomes impatient and moves early.

The Baseline Player | Set up the net player

The second baseline player strategy is to hit shots that set up your partner to hit a winning volley from the net. This is a cooperative approach that requires teamwork. As the baseline player, you're doing your best to make your partner look good.

This strategy is common at all levels of play and works particularly well when your team possesses a strong baseline player and an aggressive net player.

Patience and consistency are key attributes for a baseline player using this strategy. If your partner trusts that you'll keep the ball in play, he'll have the confidence to wait for the right opportunity to poach.

Deep, penetrating shots put pressure on the opposing baseline player. It's these types of shots that lead to a weak return that your partner can intercept.

- Hit crosscourt deep and wide.
- Hit hard and low down the middle, avoiding the net player.
- Hit crosscourt deep and high, using topspin to the backhand side.
- Hit a short-angle crosscourt that challenges the opposing baseline player to move forward.
- Lob over net player.

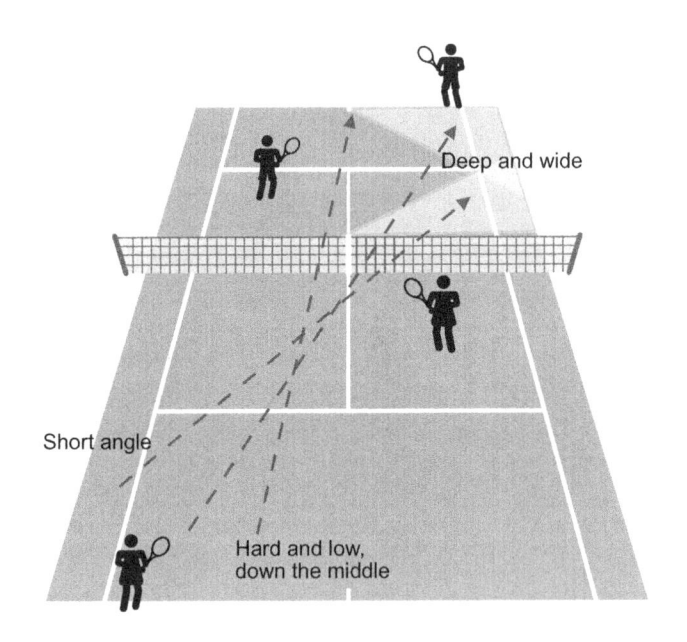

3.3.7 Playing with the intention of setting up your partner is a different mindset than if you're trying to win the point from the baseline. Even though the shots you hit may be similar, you're always considering what shot will most likely set up your partner.

The Baseline Player | How to set up your partner at net

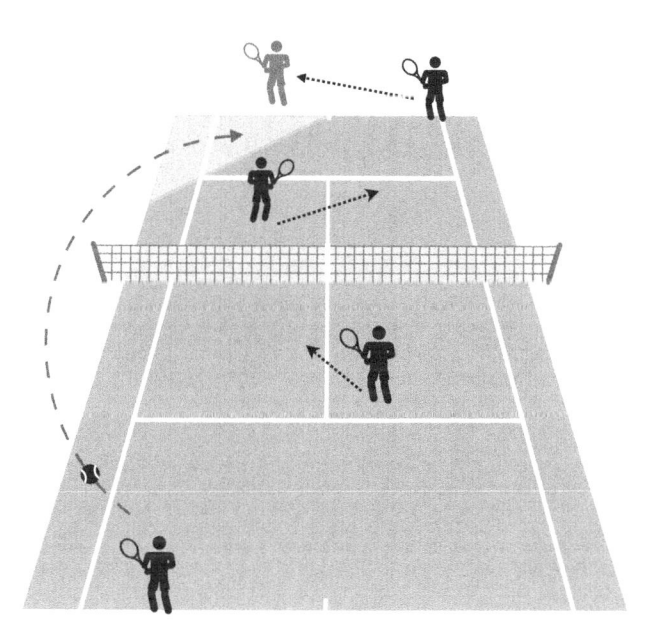

3.3.8 Lob over the net player. If the lob is challenging for the opposing baseline player, your partner has a good opportunity to poach.

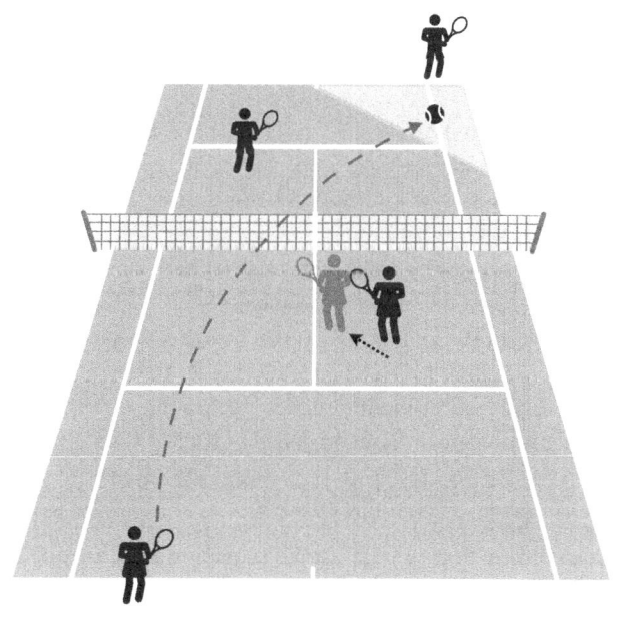

3.3.9 Hit crosscourt offensively, deep and high. The net player in the near court is anticipating a poach because the high bounce to the opposing player's backhand makes it likely he'll hit a weak shot.

The Baseline Player | Baseline player moves to the net

The third baseline player strategy is to join your partner at net. Playing both up at net is the main focus of Chapter 4.

Even if you prefer to play from the baseline in the one-up and one-back formation, there are times when you'll be "drawn in" to the offense zone by your opponent's short ball.

When moving forward to hit a short ball:
- Slow down before hitting the ball.
- Don't hit the ball too far, as you have less distance available to hit into when you're closer to the net.
- Aim the ball inside the singles sideline so you're less likely to get a difficult angled shot back.

If you end up near the service line after hitting a short ball, don't try to get back to your baseline home, as you're likely to get caught in the transition zone as your opponent hits the ball. Instead, continue to move in until you're just in front of the service line. Play out the point from this new home in the offense zone, keeping the ball crosscourt. Don't come in too far so you can still cover a lob.

3.3.10 Have the courage to stay up at net after you're drawn in by a short ball. Hold your ground and act like you belong there even if it feels unfamiliar.

The Baseline Player | Trust and adjust

3.3.11 Trust your partner. Avoid moving toward the middle to back your partner up when he's poaching. It will put you out of balance and you'll be in the wrong position if his poach is returned.

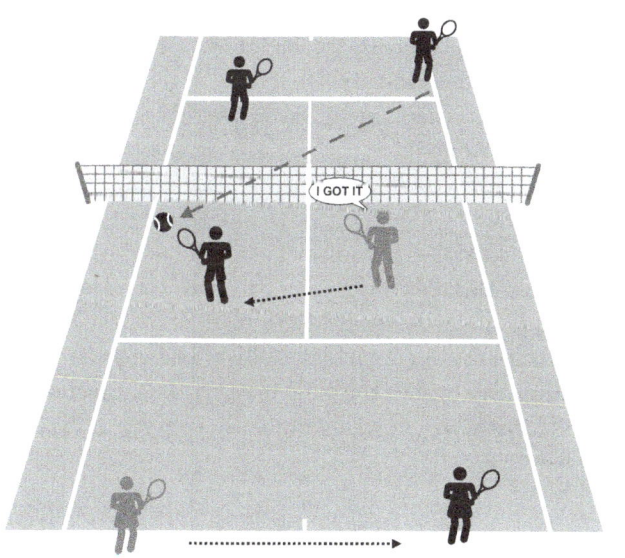

3.3.12 Adjust to your partner. If he crosses to the other side to take a short ball (as shown here) or after a poach, automatically switch to cover the side he just left. He doesn't have to tell you to "switch" because you can see that he's moved to the other side.

The Baseline Player | Troubleshooting

If you're losing the majority of points playing from the baseline, either through errors or by setting up the opposing net player, change something. There are a number of things you can do.

- Use more variety in your shots. Use different heights, speeds and spins.
- Hit to your baseline opponent's weaker side whenever you can.
- Hit toward the opposing net player if he's the weaker player. Discreetly warn your partner if you plan to do this so he can be ready to defend.
- Change the direction of the rally by lobbing over the net player or start the point in Australian formation.
- Play both back so your partner can help you at the baseline.

When receiving a difficult ball, resist the urge to hit a down-the-line shot. This is exactly what the opposing team wants you to do.

- Hit a low crosscourt lob to keep the ball out of the opposing net player's reach.
- Lob the ball up high and deep enough so the net player can't hit a strong overhead.
- If you can't lob, do whatever you can to get the ball over the net. Even if it travels to the net player, there's always a chance he'll make an error.

3.3.13 When receiving a very difficult ball, do what you can to stay in the point. If you send up a high defensive lob, your partner should join you at the baseline to help defend.

The Baseline Player | Key points

Centering Moment
- Center yourself, face the ball, and split step at the baseline home as your opponent hits the ball.
- If you don't have time to recover to your home, split step wherever you are when your opponent hits.

Receiving Phase
- If you think the ball is coming to you, decide whether to use your forehand or backhand and move in the appropriate direction.
- Be ready to take the middle ball if your partner lets it go through.
- As you focus on the ball coming toward you, take a moment to widen your gaze to assess where your opponents are positioned.
- Always let the ball bounce when you're playing from your correct baseline home.

Sending Phase
- Focus on hitting deep crosscourt groundstrokes.
- Vary the height, speed, direction, depth and spin of your shots.
- If you often get caught in the transition zone as your opponent hits, make more effort to recover to your baseline home after you hit each ball.
- Don't spectate after hitting your shot. Recover to your home immediately after your follow-through.

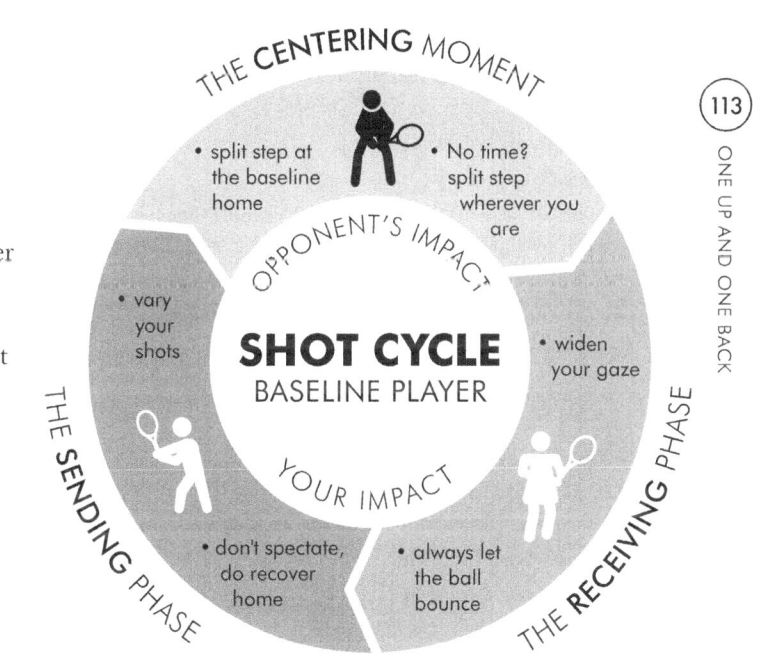

SHOT CYCLE — BASELINE PLAYER

THE CENTERING MOMENT — OPPONENT'S IMPACT
- split step at the baseline home
- No time? split step wherever you are

THE RECEIVING PHASE
- widen your gaze
- always let the ball bounce

YOUR IMPACT — THE SENDING PHASE
- don't spectate, do recover home
- vary your shots

3.4 The Lob

The lob is an essential doubles shot. Learning to lob and defend against the lob in the one-up and one-back formation develops specific skills and a communication system that will be used when playing either both up or both back (Chapter 4).

One of the advantages of the one-up and one-back formation is that the baseline player can cover all of the deep lobs. Even so, lobbing over the opposing net player in one up and one back can be an effective tactic.

Lob over the net player when:
- you're receiving a ball that's not too difficult;
- you're hitting from the side (forehand or backhand) from which you prefer to lob;
- the net player is short or standing close to the net;
- the baseline player doesn't move well laterally or has difficulty with high balls;
- you want to change the rally from a crosscourt to down-the-line direction.

Ensure the lob stays in by aiming about halfway between the baseline and service line. You don't have to hit a winning lob. It's better to have the net player reach the lob than for it to land out.

3.4.1 When playing against right-handed opponents, a lob from the deuce side travels over the net player's backhand side and lands on the backhand side of the baseline player who crosses over to cover it. This makes it more difficult for the opponents than a lob sent from the ad side.

The Lob | The magic moment

The lob over the net player can be deliberately set up as an aggressive play. This play is only used when the lobbing team remains in the one-up and one-back formation. It doesn't work if the baseline player approaches the net after the lob (see diagrams 4.2.8a and 4.2.8b).

Step 1: Lob

The Team A baseline player lobs over the opposing net player.

Step 2: Switch

As the opponents switch sides, the Team B baseline player momentarily loses sight of the Team A net player as his partner crosses in front of him.

Step 3: Terminate

At this "magic moment," the net player of Team A sneaks to the middle of the court, ready to attack a weak return with an overhead or volley. He positions himself far enough from the net to smash a lob return but can still move forward to attack a shorter ball with a volley.

Step 4: Recover

If Team A's net player does not hit the ball, the magic moment has passed and he's once again responsible for his original side.

3.4.2 Notice how the baseline player in the far court loses sight of the opposing net player as his partner crosses in front of him. This is the magic moment when the net player in the near court can move to the middle.

The Lob | Effective crosscourt lobs

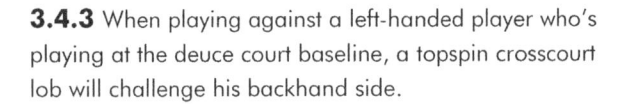

3.4.3 When playing against a left-handed player who's playing at the deuce court baseline, a topspin crosscourt lob will challenge his backhand side.

3.4.4 If you're left-handed, use the same tactic when you're hitting from the ad side. Your forehand topspin lob will challenge the opposing baseline player's backhand.

The Lob | Mine or yours?

When defending against a lob, verbal communication between partners is essential. Even experienced partners benefit from expressing their intentions.

As the net player, you have first dibs on whether or not you take a lob. A short lob is best taken by the net player. Assess and make a quick decision about whether you'll hit the lob as an overhead. If the lob is easily in your range, call "mine" and hit it. The safest target is into the diamond target area.

- If you don't like to talk just before hitting, show your intention with clear body language.
- If your partner has called "mine" to cover a lob that ends up being easily in your range, go ahead and hit it.
- If you have to run forward to hit your overhead, take care with your shot. It's easy to hit this ball long.

Let your partner cover the lob if you have to move back more than two or three steps. As a guideline, leave the ball for your partner if you'll be hitting the ball behind the service line. Call "yours" or "help" to alert your partner if he hasn't already called for the lob.

3.4.5 As net player, be clear whether you intend to hit the lob or not. If you have claimed the lob, don't back out. Your partner has enough time to cover the lob only if you give him adequate warning.

The Lob | Mine or yours? What not to do

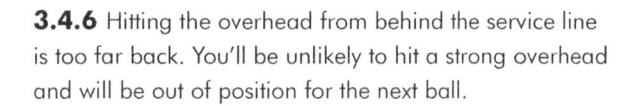

3.4.6 Hitting the overhead from behind the service line is too far back. You'll be unlikely to hit a strong overhead and will be out of position for the next ball.

3.4.7 When you're unclear about whether you plan to hit the lob as the net player, it's tempting for the your partner to move toward the middle to back you up. This puts your team out of position no matter who hits the ball.

The Lob | Covering with a switch

When covering a lob that travels over the net player, the baseline player is responsible for making and communicating the decision about whether to switch sides. As the baseline player, you have a better view of where the lob will land and you're the player responsible for hitting it.

Communicate your decision immediately by making the verbal command "got it, switch" or just "switch."

Run diagonally back to get into the best position to hit the lob. Prepare early by turning sideways and running with your racquet back. Your best options are to drive the ball down the line, lob crosscourt or, as a last resort, hit a high lob down the middle.

The net player immediately moves diagonally to switch back to opposite-side service line. This switch back to the service line is important so he's a safe distance from the opposite net player and can defend if your shot is weak. If you're obviously struggling to retrieve a difficult lob, your partner should switch all the way back to the baseline.

There'll be times when you play with a partner who doesn't communicate whether or not you should switch. In this case, as the net player, you'll have to make your own decision.

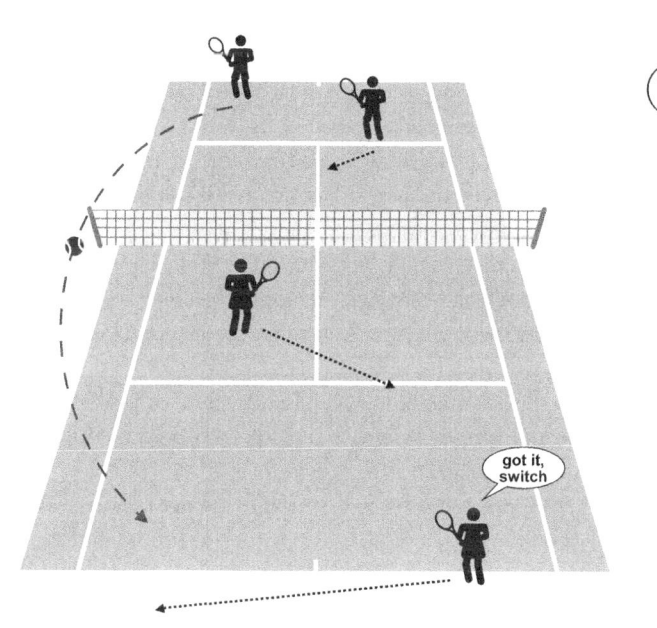

3.4.8 The switch back movement of the net player resembles the zigzag segment in a steep trail, called a "switchback."

The Lob | Covering with a stay

When a lob is traveling over the middle of the court, the baseline player needs to make and communicate the decision about whether to switch or not. When the switch isn't necessary, it's called a stay.

If the ball travels anywhere between the inside shoulder of the net player to the outside doubles sideline on the baseline player's side, there's no need to switch. Staying takes away any advantage the opposing team might gain from a switch, including the opportunity for them to execute the the "magic moment" play (diagram 3.4.2).

- As the baseline player, call "got it, stay" or just "stay" promptly and clearly when a lob travels down the middle of the court.
- When the lob is near the middle, the net player should move a couple of steps toward the sideline to give you more room to hit your shot.
- Hit crosscourt toward the opposing baseline player. If the opposing net player has moved toward the middle in anticipation of a switch, hit down his alley.
- Both you and your partner need to recover to your respective one up and one back homes by the time the ball bounces in the opponents' court.

3.4.9 As the baseline player, you're responsible for commanding the switch or stay promptly and loud enough so your partner can hear. However, if the lob is obviously crosscourt, you don't need to say anything.

3.5 Playing Straight

Playing straight is the down-the-line variation of the one-up and one-back formation. It can occur after a lob has forced one team to switch sides or when a point is started with Australian, I formation or a planned poach.

Playing-straight one up and one back is worth considering separately, as the positioning and tactics differ significantly from the usual crosscourt pattern.

Both the baseline and net players are lined up directly across from each other.

The point is played out between baseline players in a down-the-line direction. Both of their homes are closer to the center mark than usual as they don't have to cover the angles that are available in a crosscourt rally.

The net players move near or across the center line as they attempt to poach and both of their homes are close to this line. From here they can be actively involved in the point, which is taking place primarily on the baseline players' half of the court.

3.5.1 Most players do not think about practicing the down-the-line variation of one up and one back. Learning how to play it effectively can give you an advantage.

Playing Straight | Net player's home

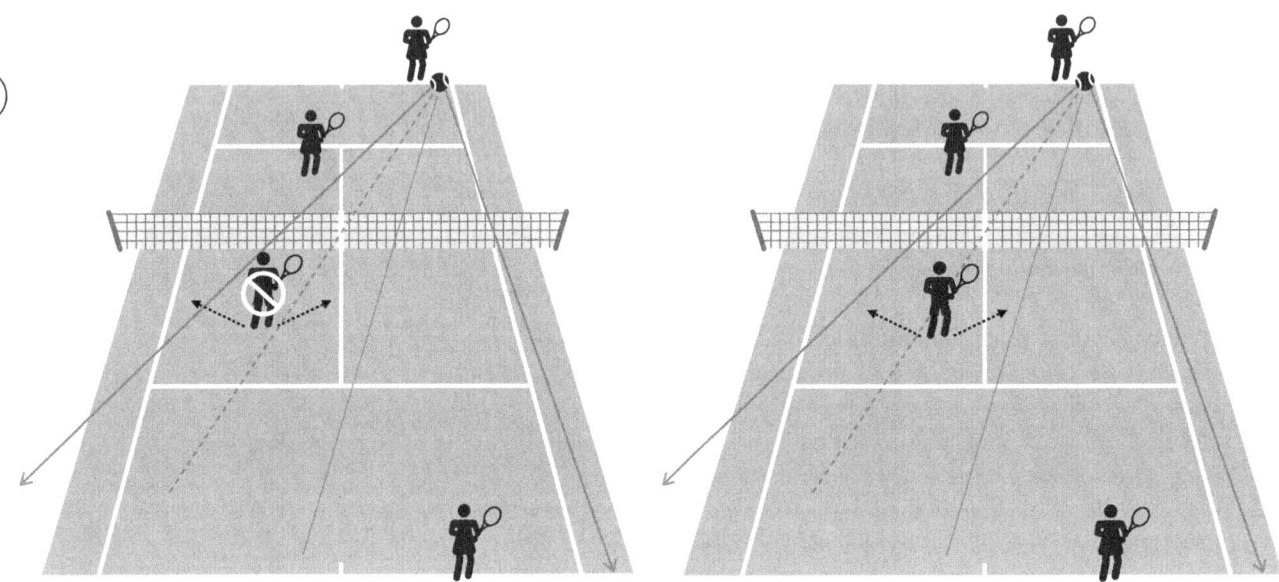

3.5.2 As the net player, your usual home in the center of the service box is incorrect. Standing there, you're essentially out of the play, opening up a hole in the middle and leaving too much of the court for your partner to cover.

3.5.3 Your correct home is now near the center line. From here you'll need to stay alert for poaching opportunities on the middle ball and be ready to move diagonally forward to cut off a short-angle crosscourt.

Playing Straight | Baseline player's home

3.5.4 As the baseline player, your correct home when playing straight is behind the baseline, about halfway between the center mark and the doubles sideline. This puts you in the best position to cover your area.

3.5.5 In contrast, notice how in crosscourt one up and one back, your home is farther over in order to cover the angles available to the opposing baseline player.

Playing Straight | The defense-in-offense method

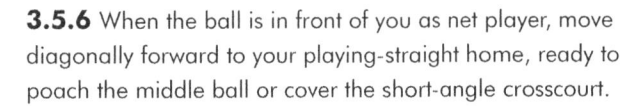

3.5.6 When the ball is in front of you as net player, move diagonally forward to your playing-straight home, ready to poach the middle ball or cover the short-angle crosscourt.

3.5.7 When the ball is behind you, move back. From here you're in a better position to defend the opposing net player's poach and you're not in the way if your partner wants to hit a short-angle crosscourt.

Playing Straight | Baseline player on deuce is better

When playing straight, the team with the baseline player on the deuce side is usually in the more favorable arrangement. The baseline player has his forehand (FH) on the outside and can use it to drive the ball deep to the opposing baseline player's backhand (BH). The net player has his forehand on the inside. This is advantageous because the forehand volley provides farther reach than a backhand and tends to be the stronger side.

The team with the baseline player on the ad side is usually in the less favorable arrangement as the baseline player has his backhand on the outside and net player has his backhand on the inside.

Whenever a team includes a left-handed player, however, playing straight on the ad side becomes more beneficial, especially if the team has practiced this formation and developed tactics to benefit from the lefty's forehand shots.

When playing straight with the baseline player on the ad side, the lefty's forehand volley is on the inside and can come as a surprise to the other team, especially if he's aggressive. When the lefty is on the baseline, his forehand is on the outside, which lines up with the opposite baseline player's forehand.

3.5.8 Be very active at net when playing straight. You can cross over the center line to poach so long as you move back when the ball is behind you.

Playing Straight | How to set it up

3.5.9 Playing ad-court Australian will lead to playing straight with the baseline player on the deuce side, which is the more favorable arrangement. This is one of the reasons why Australian is played more often serving from the ad than the deuce side.

3.5.10 A lob over the net player from the deuce side will set up playing straight with the baseline player on the deuce side. This is usually the more favorable arrangement.

Playing Straight | Baseline player tactics

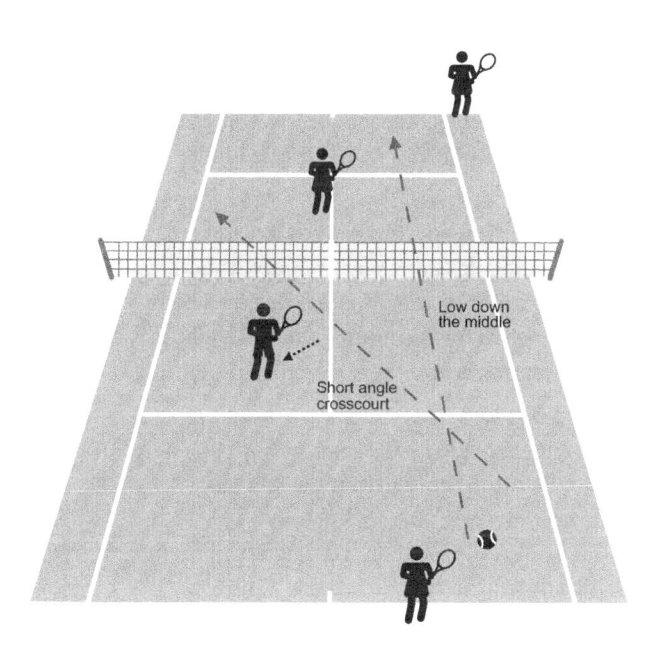

3.5.11 As the baseline player on the deuce side, use your forehand to pressure the opposing baseline player's backhand. Once he's pulled out wide, hit low down the middle or a short-angle crosscourt. Here there's enough space to hit the short-angle shot because your partner at net has moved back correctly when the ball is behind him.

3.5.12 To get out of playing straight, send a crosscourt lob over the net player. The opponents will switch, and play continues in the usual crosscourt one up and one back.

One Up and One Back | Summary

One up and one back is the foundation for the other playing formations. If you're a tennis beginner or a singles player who's new to doubles, take the time to develop a consistent and effective one-up and one-back game before investing a lot of time into learning and practicing the both-up formation.

The Net Player

- Learn to hit your volleys into the diamond-shaped target from your forehand and backhand on both ad and deuce sides.
- Know your correct home and commit to being there by the time your opponent hits the ball.
- Only use the defense-in-offense method if you can move forward to your correct home in time.
- Cover your alley without compromising your ability to poach the middle ball.

The Baseline Player

- The baseline player's home is behind the baseline. Always let the ball bounce when playing from here.
- Hit deep, penetrating crosscourt groundstrokes with the intention of winning the point from the baseline or setting your partner up to hit a winning volley from the net.
- Keep the ball away from the opposing net player unless the net player is noticeably weak at net.
- Use a down-the-line shot only when you're well set-up, never when you're under pressure.

The Lob

- Take the time to learn how to lob and integrate it into your game. It's an essential doubles shot.
- The baseline player should cover the deep lobs and is responsible for communicating "switch" or "stay" to the net player.

Playing Straight

- Playing straight is a one-up and one-back variation that has different positioning and tactics than crosscourt one up and one back.
- The point is played out between the baseline players in a down-the-line direction.
- The baseline player's home is about halfway between the center mark and doubles sideline, and the net player's home is close to the center line.
- The team with the baseline player on the deuce side is generally in the more favorable arrangement.

CHAPTER 4

In the Zone

4.1 Playing in the Same Zone

In "both up" and "both back" formations, both partners play from within the same zone. This eliminates the gap between you and your partner, which is the main disadvantage of the one-up and one-back formation.

Playing both up offers many opportunities to win points. A skilled team that likes to play at net will do everything they can to get both players into the offense zone before their opponents.

- Volleys and overheads can be hit with precision and power and these are the shots you use most often from the offense zone.
- When you hit volleys and overheads you take time away from your opponents because the ball doesn't bounce before you hit it.
- Being close to net opens up more opportunities to hit angled shots that your opponents can't reach.
- When you hit your volley from inside the attack zone, you can hit down on the ball, making it more likely that you'll hit a winning shot.

Both back is the best way to defend against a team entrenched in the offense zone. A skilled team can win many points playing both back, even though it's a defensive formation.

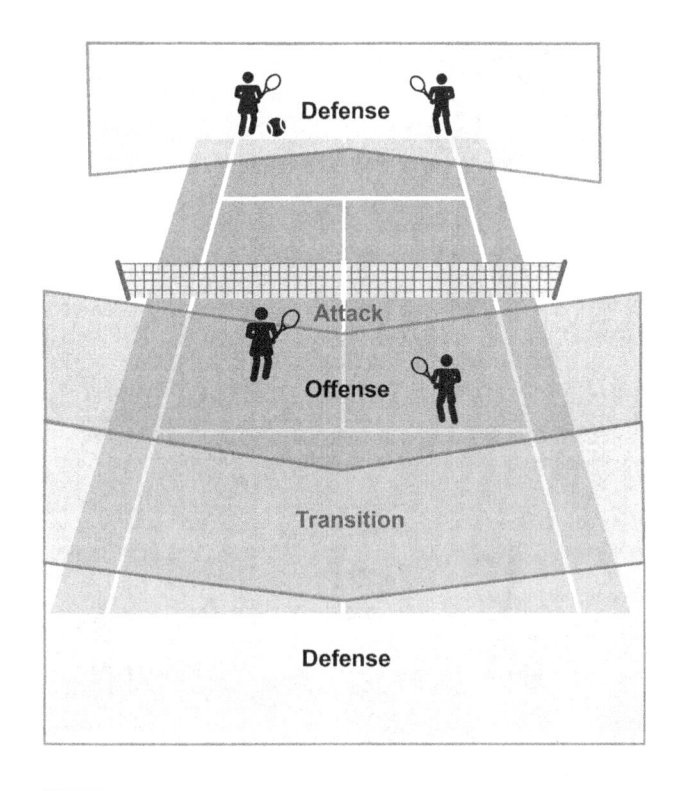

4.1.1 When you play in the same zone as your partner, either offense or defense, you eliminate the gap between you and your partner where the opponent can put a ball away.

Playing in the Same Zone | Joining your partner

The rules of tennis dictate that each point begins with the Server and Receiver starting back. The Server must serve from behind the baseline. The Receiver must let the ball bounce before making the return. Most Receivers choose a starting location well behind the service line and, depending on the likelihood of a hard or deep serve, may start from behind the baseline.

To get into a both-up formation, the Server or Receiver moves from her starting location, through the transition zone, to the offense zone. The shot that provides this transition is an "approach shot." When both the Server and Receiver join their partners in their offense zones it creates a new formation called "dogfight."

The easiest way to get into a both-back formation is for Server's Partner or Receiver's Partner to start back. However, unless there's a good reason to start in the defense zone, both back usually occurs as a defensive response to the opponents moving into the offense zone.

The movement from the offense zone to the defense zone is like a reverse approach shot. As with its counterpart, the approach shot, it requires awareness and planning to execute without getting caught in the wrong position.

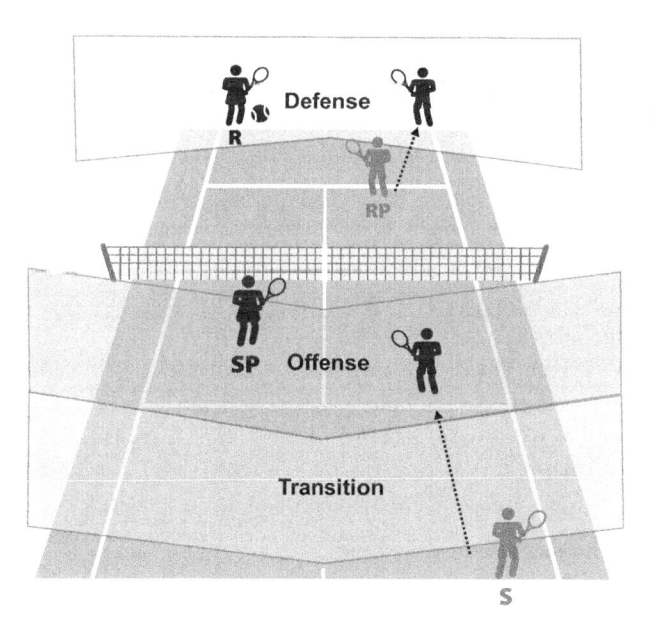

4.1.2 Unless your team has started the point both back, you have to move through the transition zone to join your partner. Time your movement so that you reach a home in the defense or offense zone before your opponent hits the ball.

Playing in the Same Zone | The wall

The traditional method of positioning when both partners are at net is called "the wall." With this method, partners line up side by side in the offense zone, always maintaining the same distance from each other. There are two main problems with the wall positioning.

Who takes the lob?

There is no obvious answer to this dilemma. Teams have to figure it out for themselves. Some suggestions include:
- Players cover their own half of the court.
- The faster or the taller player covers the deep lobs.
- The player who gets behind the service line first takes the lob.
- Both players play back far enough to cover lobs.

Who takes the middle ball?

The usual suggestion is that the player with the forehand volley in the middle takes the middle ball.
- This, however, isn't necessarily the player who's in the best position to put the ball away.
- It also doesn't make sense for teams with a left-handed player, as both forehands or both backhands will always be in the middle.

4.1.3 When using the wall method, players are advised to move "like windshield wipers," sliding left and right depending on the position of the ball in the opponents' court. However, this system tends to lead to confusion about who should take the shot when faced with deep lobs and middle balls.

Playing in the Same Zone | Staggered offense

"Staggered offense" is a modern system of both-up positioning that works well for all levels of recreational players. Both partners play in the offense zone with one partner staggered diagonally behind the other. Lower level or less agile players will stagger more than higher level players or those with advanced movement skills.

Gigi Fernandez, a 17-time Grand Slam Doubles Champion, uses the staggered formation in her coaching program for recreational players, the "Gigi Method" (doubles.tv). Gigi says that she's actually covered the net this way since she was a developing junior. She points out that all great professional doubles teams use this system. You won't necessarily see them staggering, because they're so quick and agile that covering lobs isn't an issue. However, they're always aware of the stagger in their minds and know which player should attack the middle ball and who is responsible for the lob (personal communication, 2019).

I initially came across the staggered system in Helle Sparre's book *Dynamite Doubles* (2004). She describes how, as a professional player, she moved and positioned herself instinctively. After she began teaching recreational players, she carefully studied her own game, analyzing how she moved and thought while playing each point. From this research she developed her teaching method, the "Dynamite Doubles System."

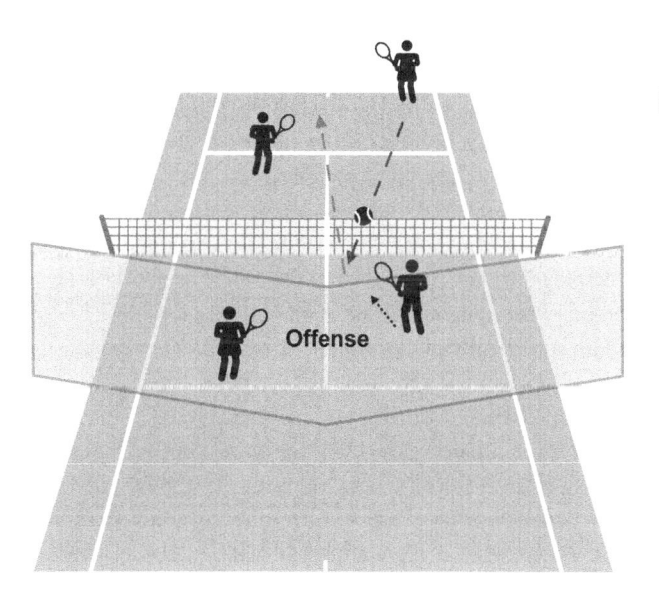

4.1.4 Staggered offense makes it clear which partner is responsible for the lob and the middle ball. Here the player on the deuce side has first dibs on the middle ball and is in the best position to put it away between the two opposing players. The player on the ad side will back her up in the middle if needed and is also responsible for covering deep lobs.

Playing in the Same Zone | Workhorse and terminator

The Workhorse and Terminator are the two clearly defined roles in the staggered-offense system. These names were coined by Helle Sparre in her book *Dynamite Doubles* (2004). Other coaches or players may use different names for the same roles.

The location of the ball in the opponents' court determines who plays which role. The Terminator is the player directly across from the ball. The Workhorse is the player diagonal to the ball. Unless a doubles team specifically plans otherwise, each partner plays Workhorse and Terminator approximately the same amount of time over the course of a match.

The Terminator plays close to the net and is therefore in a good position to poach and put away the middle ball. She can safely play close to the net because her partner, the Workhorse, is staggered behind her and covers the majority of shots, including the deep lobs. These roles are covered in detail in the Workhorse (4.3) and Terminator (4.4) sections.

This system is deceptively simple in theory. During play, however, things move quickly and the roles can switch during a point depending on where the ball is in the opponents' end of the court. With practice, repetition and experience, where to move when playing the staggered-offense system becomes natural.

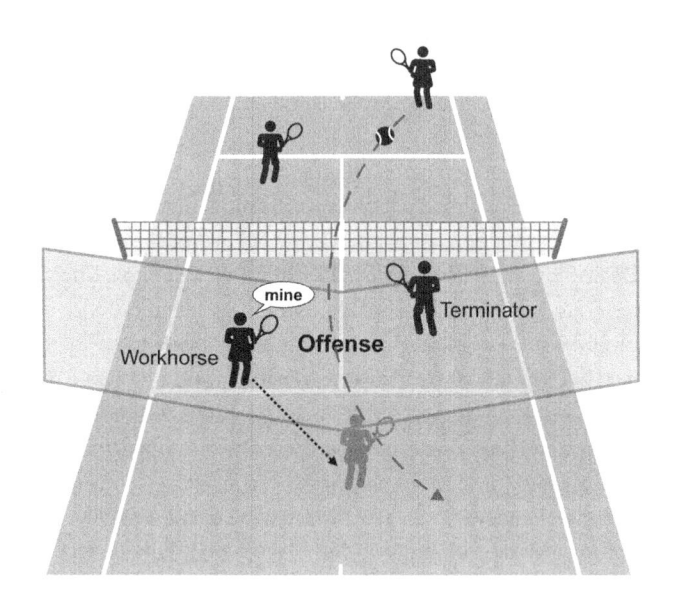

4.1.5 Each partner has specific jobs with clear responsibilities. The Terminator can play close to the net, where it's easier to put the ball away, because she trusts her Workhorse partner to cover the deep lobs.

Playing in the Same Zone | Location of homes

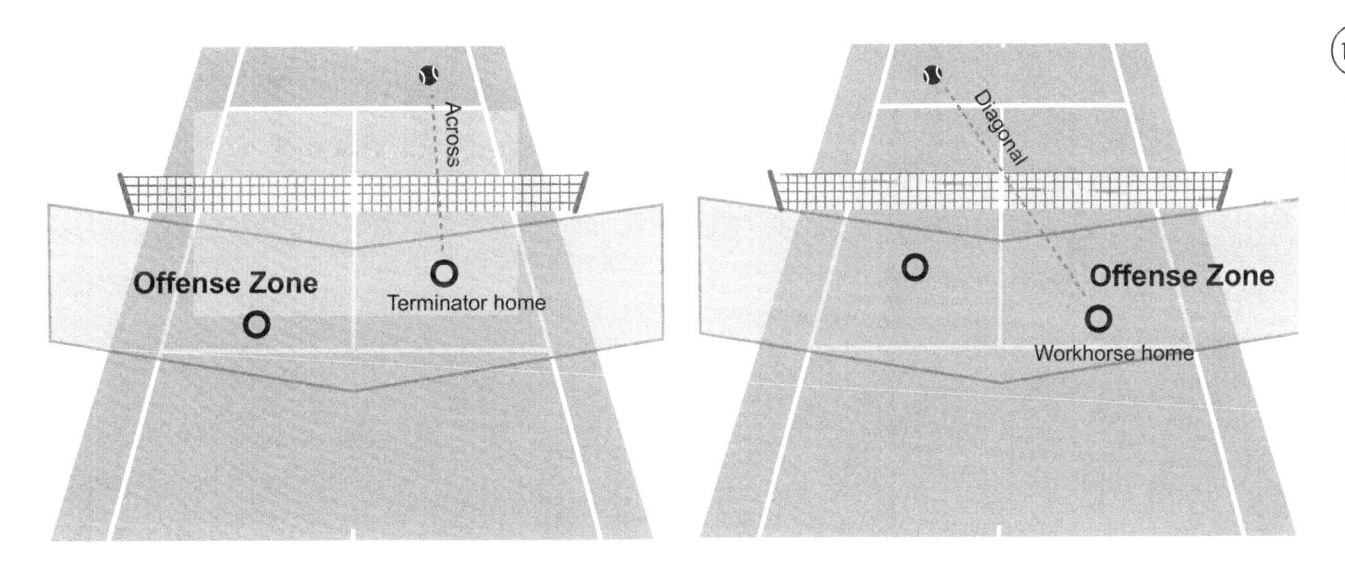

4.1.6 You're the Terminator when you're directly across from the ball that's in your opponents' end of the court. Notice that the Terminator and the ball are in the same vertical half of the court. Your usual home is in the middle of the service box. This home is closer to the ball than the Workhorse home.

4.1.7 You're the Workhorse when you're diagonal to the ball that's in the opponents' end of the court. Your usual home is about one step in from the service line and approximately equal distance from the center line and singles sideline. Your home is farther away from the ball than the Terminator home.

Playing in the Same Zone | Remember your role

4.1.8 When learning staggered offense, it helps to remind yourself of your probable role before you start each point. The Server or Receiver will usually become the Workhorse. For example, if you're the Server and you approach the net with a crosscourt shot, you'll be the Workhorse and your partner will be the Terminator.

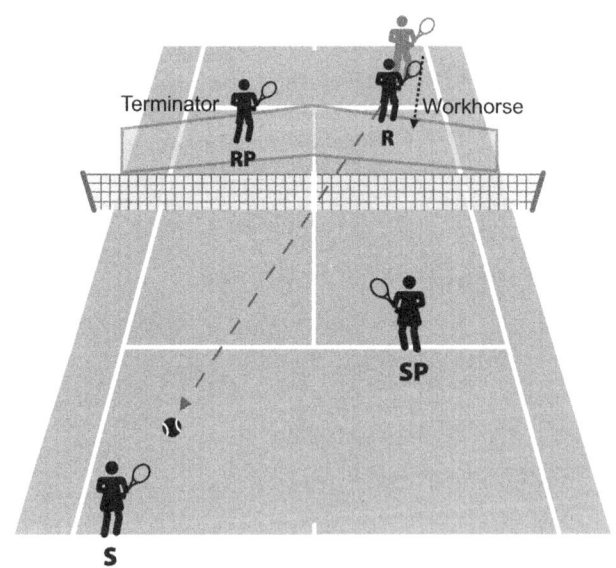

4.1.9 In the staggered-offense system, as long as the approach shot is hit crosscourt, Server's Partner or Receiver's Partner will become the Terminator. For example, if you're Receiver's Partner and your partner approaches the net with a crosscourt shot, you'll be the Terminator and your partner will be the Workhorse.

Playing in the Same Zone | Two against one

A both-up team playing against a one-up and one-back team is in an ideal situation.* Once the baseline player has joined her partner in the offense zone and made a successful first volley, it's like playing two against one.

A simple and effective offensive tactic is called "pick and stick." The both-up team picks on the baseline player, keeping the ball deep and moving her side to side. As soon as the Terminator has an opportunity, she "sticks" it to the opposite net player, hitting at or behind her.

When faced with a both-up team, many players think the best solution is for the remaining baseline player to move into the net. In fact, there's rarely enough time to move in and get into a good position before the offensive team hits the next volley.

A better solution, as the one-up and one-back net player, is to move back and join your partner in the defense zone. You'll need to carefully choose your opportunity to move back to avoid getting caught in the transition zone. Once you have joined your partner in the defense zone you can be of help rather than being a target. Playing both back is covered in section 4.8.

---

* Gigi Fernandez assigns descriptive names for each of the teams in this particular arrangement (doubles.tv). "The Holy Grail" portrays the advantage of the both-up team, while "The Highway to Hell" depicts the situation of the one-up and one-back team.

4.1.10 Both up against one up and one back is like playing one against two for the lone player at the baseline. The offensive team "picks" on the baseline player, keeping the ball deep so she has little time to react. When the baseline player is eventually forced into hitting a weak ball, the Terminator moves forward and "sticks" it to the opposite net player.

4.2 The Approach Shot

Once you have developed consistent groundstrokes and volleys, and understand the one-up and one-back formation, you're ready to learn to join your partner at net. An "approach shot" is the ball you hit to facilitate your move from the defense to offense zone. This section covers six different approach shots.

In doubles, most approach shots are planned, and you commit to moving in before you see the effectiveness of your shot. The easiest way to get into the net is to approach on a short ball you can hit from inside the transition zone. This gives you enough time to get centered at the Workhorse home before your opponent hits the ball.

1. Crosscourt approach
2. Getting drawn in
3. Return and approach (regular or chip-and-charge variation)

When hitting any of these three approach shots:
- Slow down as you hit the ball.
- Hit from a position where both feet are inside the transition zone.
- After you hit the approach shot, continue moving forward to your Workhorse home in the offense zone.

The quality of the approach shot has a big effect on the outcome of the point.
- Hit the shot low and/or deep, being careful to avoid the net player.
- Keep it within the singles lines to take away your opponent's ability to hit strongly angled shots.
- Both slice and topspin shots can make effective approach shots.

There are other ways to get into net that don't depend on your opponent hitting a short ball. Each of these options require you to hit a very particular shot that allows you to move in.

4. Serve and volley
5. The lob
6. The sneak

With all six of these approach shot options, you're most vulnerable on the first shot you hit after you move in, as you're still getting set up in your new home. Getting centered and ready by the time your opponent hits the ball is crucial. When approaching the net, you also have to be ready to move back to cover a crosscourt lob or a lob over your partner's head. If you pay attention to your opponent's movement and racquet position, you can often anticipate what shot she's going to hit.

The Approach Shot | First volley targets

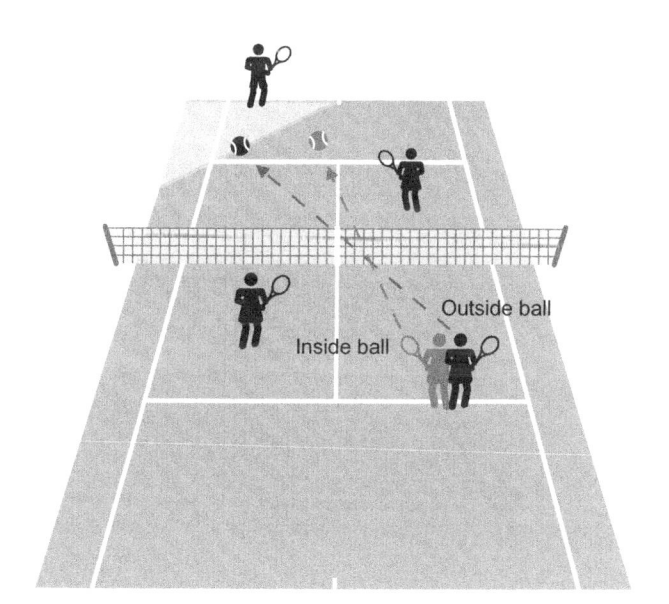

4.2.1 Hit your first volley crosscourt. The safest options are to angle an outside ball toward the alley and direct an inside ball closer to the middle. Resist the urge to hit straight at the opposite net player or down the alley unless the ball is high and slow enough that you can move in close to the net.

4.2.2 Occasionally, the opposing baseline player sends a short floater that you can charge toward and hit down on. Aim for the opposite net player's feet or down the alley and recover to the Terminator home as you're now across from the ball. Your partner moves back to the Workhorse home as she's now diagonal to the ball (see diagrams 4.3.7a and 4.3.7b).

The Approach Shot | Crosscourt approach

Approach on any ball you can hit from within the transition zone. This is easiest from a ball that lands slightly short in the court. It's also possible to move in and contact the ball at the top of the bounce when you receive a softer shot that isn't necessarily short. A third variation is to hit a swinging volley before the ball bounces.

On all crosscourt approach shots:
- Slow down before you hit the ball.
- Keep your eyes on the ball and your center of gravity low as you hit.
- Your ideal target is deep crosscourt, landing within the singles lines.
- Continue to move forward to your Workhorse home in the offense zone, in time to split step as the opponent strikes the ball.

You want to get your approach shot in the court while making it challenging enough so the baseline player can't easily pass or lob you. Topspin or slice may be used, depending on what shots you have available in your repertoire. Topspin helps to keep the ball in. Slice travels more slowly and keeps the ball low, which gives you more time to move forward and makes your opponent hit up on her return.

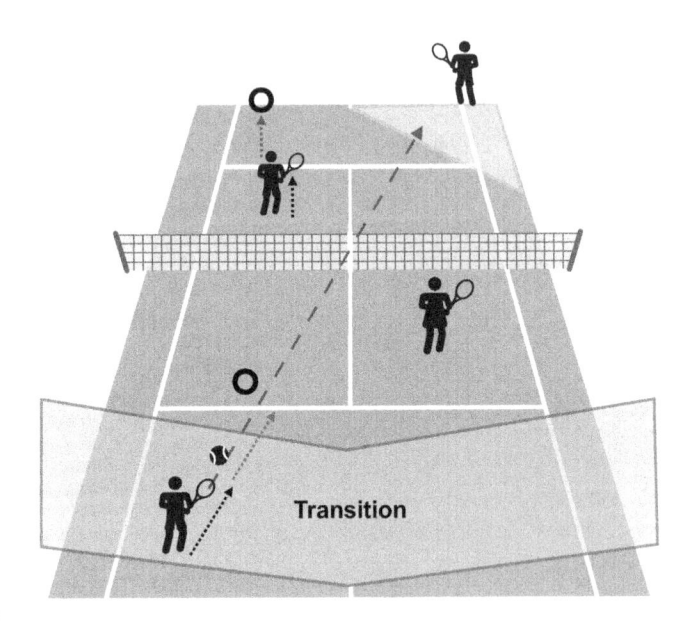

4.2.3 Hit crosscourt approach shots from inside the transition zone, slowing down as you make contact. After you hit, continue moving forward to your Workhorse home. The best defense for the opposing team is for the net player to move back to the service line or baseline (see diagrams 4.8.4 to 4.8.5b).

The Approach Shot | Getting drawn in

Getting "drawn in" is when your opponent hits you a ball so short that you end up hitting it from within the offense zone. When this happens, stay up and make your way to the Workhorse home after you have hit your shot. You don't have time to get back to your baseline home, even if you prefer playing from the baseline.

Your opponent may have intentionally drawn you in or she may have mis-hit the ball.

- Even if you have to sprint to reach the ball, slow down before making contact.
- Do your best to hit crosscourt, avoiding the net player and lifting the ball up to clear the net.
- The distance to the baseline is shorter when you hit from inside the service line. Be careful not to send this ball too far.
- Don't get cute and try to lob a short ball over the net player. There's not enough space available to hit into.

If the ball you're receiving is very angled, consider sending a short-angled return (see diagram 5.2.4, Cat and Mouse). Move in farther than usual after you have hit, as your opponent is likely to send a short-angle shot back.

4.2.4 You might decide to intentionally draw your opponent in if she plays poorly at net or if your opponents are obviously uncomfortable playing both up.

The Approach Shot | Return and approach

Approaching from the return of serve gets you into the net early in the point. When your opponents typically hit deep, the serve might be the shortest ball you'll get as, by definition, it must land within the service box.

- It's easier to approach off a serve that's short or soft, usually a second serve.
- As with the crosscourt approach, make sure both of your feet are inside the transition zone as you strike the ball. Aim crosscourt and inside the singles sideline.
- After you hit your return, continue into the Workhorse home without any hesitation. Even if you make a poor return, it's too late to get back to your home at the baseline.

If you're new to joining your partner in the offense zone, return and approach is a good place to start. With this tactic, you don't have to figure out in the middle of a rally when to approach. Just make the decision and move in on the second serve.

If you're losing points against a team who is serving and volleying, try the return and approach. You might find that you're more successful when you're all four up in the dogfight formation (see diagrams 4.5.1 to 4.5.4).

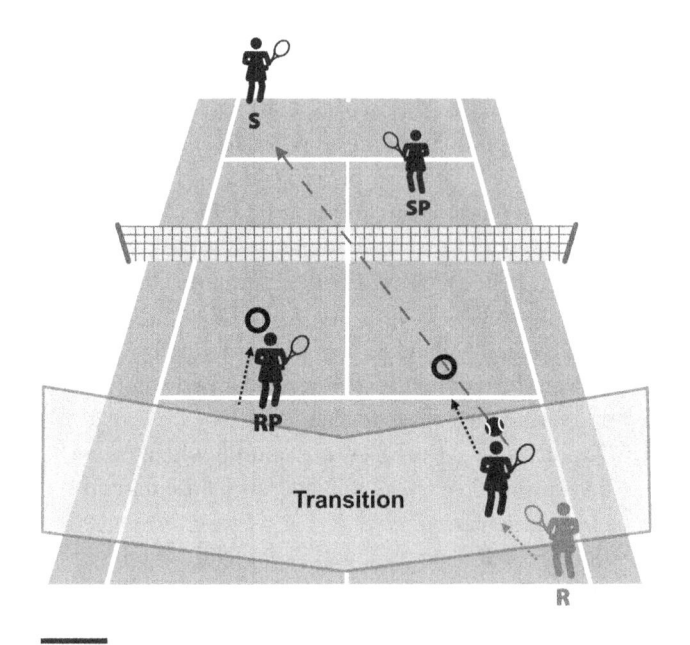

4.2.5 The return and approach is relatively easy to do on a second serve return. Make your plan before the serve is sent, visualizing where you'll hit your shot and where you'll move. You can change your mind and stay back if the serve lands too deep. You'll know the serve is too deep if you're not in the transition zone when you make contact.

The Approach Shot | Chip-and-charge variation

"Chip and charge"* is an aggressive variation of the return and approach shot. To do it, sneak well into the transition zone while the Server is in motion, split step as she hits the ball, and hit a slice return immediately after the bounce. The slice technique allows you to hit on the run and you can quickly adapt to reach high, low or angled balls.

- With chip and charge, you're fully committed to approaching the net no matter where the serve lands.
- Unless the first serve is unusually weak, it's best used on a second serve.
- Let your partner know if you plan to chip and charge. She'll need to pay extra attention to move forward to her Terminator home at the right time, as your return will pass by the Server's Partner earlier than usual.
- Chip and charge works particularly well on clay courts, where the serve slows down after the bounce and the Server has less stability to set her feet on her second shot.

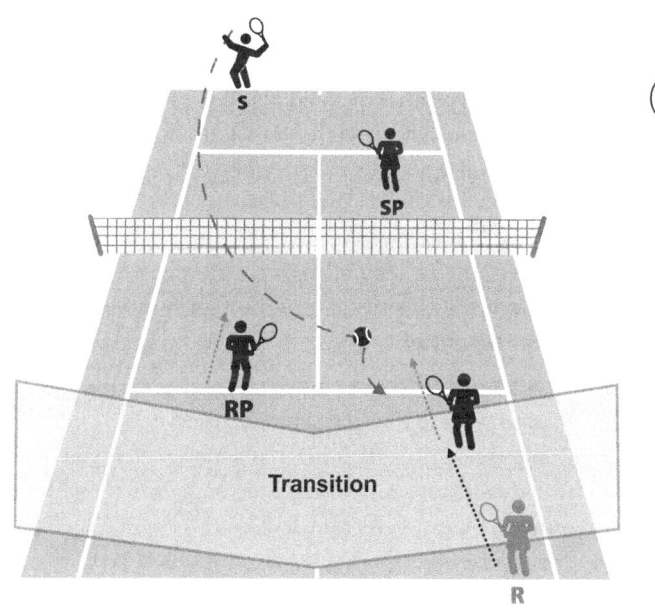

---

* "Chip" is another term for "slice," and "charge" refers to your aggressive movement toward the net as the Server is serving and after you have hit your return.

4.2.6 Chip and charge is a gutsy, relatively advanced tactic. When it goes well, your team is on top of the net, ready to pounce on the next shot before the serving team knows what's happened.

The Approach Shot | Serve and volley

The serve and volley is when you approach the net directly after your serve.

Hit your serve with spin and depth to give you time to move into the net. Powerful serves are usually not as effective because you have less time to get in before the ball bounces.

The T or body serves are good placement choices, as they limit the amount of angle the Receiver can hit. Also test out the effectiveness of the angled serve to the Receiver's backhand.

To serve and volley:
1. Plan to serve and volley before you serve.
2. Run forward directly from your serve, even if you think your serve might land long or go into the net.
3. Slow down just before the ball bounces in the service box on the other side, split stepping when the Receiver strikes the ball. You probably won't make it all the way to the service line. That's OK.
4. Move toward the oncoming ball, hitting it as a volley or half-volley, or sometimes move back to cover a lob.
5. If you aren't already at the Workhorse home, continue to move in after you hit your first volley.

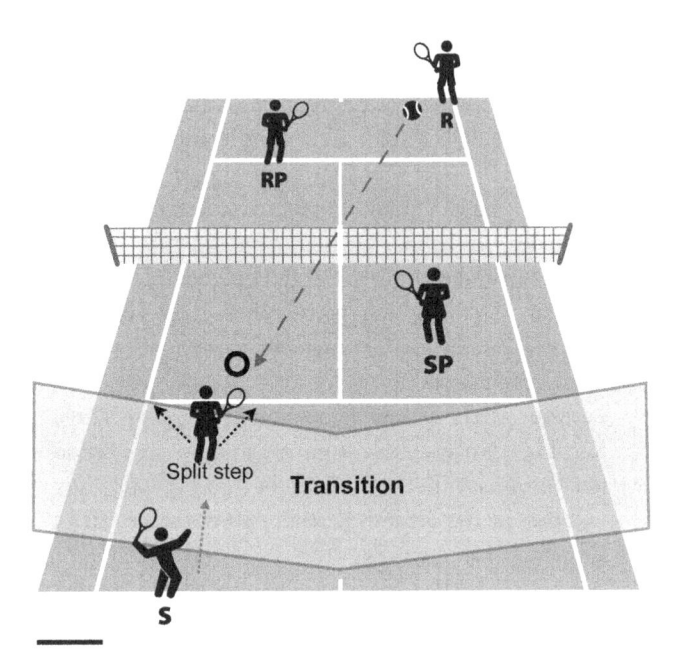

4.2.7 When you serve and volley, some of the opponent's returns will land long or wide. You'll need to refine your perception skills so you know when not to hit the first volley (see diagram 3.2.19).

The Approach Shot | The lob

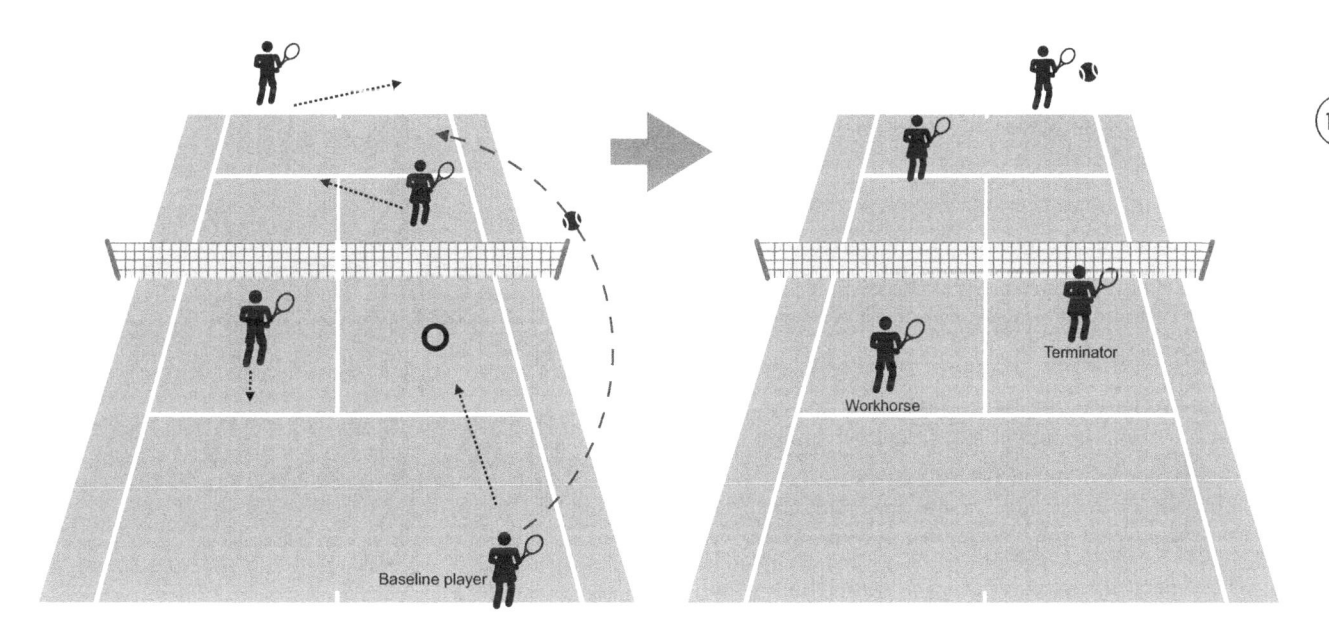

4.2.8a The lob over the net player makes a potent approach shot. It can be hit during a point or from a return of serve. When the baseline player (or Receiver) is sure that the lob will clear the net player, she runs quickly forward to the Terminator home.

4.2.8b As the baseline player runs in, her partner moves back to the Workhorse home, as she's now diagonal to the ball and responsible for covering all deep lobs.

The Approach Shot | The sneak

A sneak* approach shot is when you wait until after you see the effectiveness of your shot before moving into the net. Look for two common situations when you can sneak into the Workhorse home.

1. You hit a low-crosscourt lob.
- Once you're sure that your ball will land deep, run quickly and quietly into your Workhorse home.
- Lobs that force the baseline opponent back without being too high work the best.

2. You hit a challenging angled shot.
- If you see your opponent reaching for an angled ball, you may have enough time to sneak in.
- Sometimes you can sneak in on an angled serve, even if you weren't planning to serve and volley.

These sneak approaches can work from either the ad or deuce sides.
- Use them on the deuce side when the crosscourt baseline player has a weak forehand or is left-handed.
- If you're left-handed, sneak in from the ad side, using your topspin crosscourt forehand to hit to the opposing baseline player's backhand.

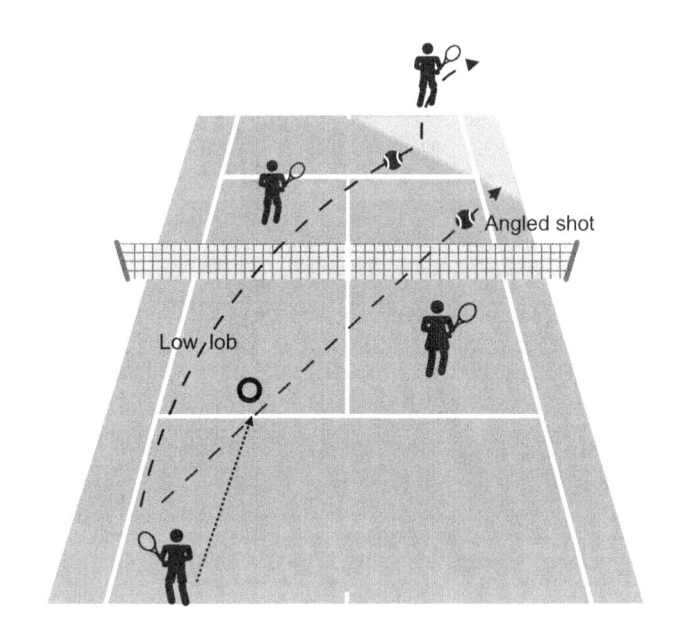

---

*The theory behind instinctual (or sneak) versus planned approach shots is considered in *Women's Tennis Tactics* (Antoun, 2007).

4.2.9 A sneak approach shot makes a nice variation and can surprise your opponent. The sneak is also known as an instinctual approach shot because you sense that you have hit a ball that will make a good approach shot before you commit to moving in.

The Approach Shot | Down-the-line approach

When you're playing the down-the-line variation of the one-up and one-back formation (see section 3.5.), you can use modifications of the different approach shots to get into a both-up formation.

When you approach down the line, you need to move forward all the way to the Terminator home after you hit your shot. Hit your approach shot deep and without too much pace, or slightly higher with topspin, to give yourself enough time to get in.

- On a short ball or if you're drawn in, hit a down-the-line approach shot, aiming deep and to the opposing baseline player's weaker side if possible.
- Aim your shot near the singles sideline so that it won't be poached.
- After hitting, recover immediately to the Terminator home. Be ready to cover a shot down your alley or poach a middle ball.
- Your partner moves diagonally back to the Workhorse home when she hears and sees you charging in. She's now responsible for all deep lobs and should be ready for this likely shot.

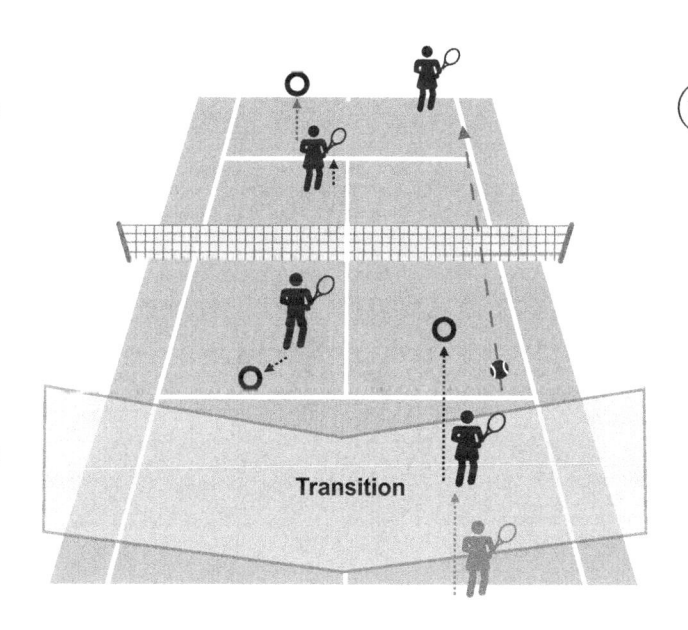

4.2.10 You'll need to be at least halfway into the transition zone as you hit the ball to make it all the way to the Terminator home. Your partner must remember to move back as she's now responsible for all the deep lobs, including those over your head.

The Approach Shot | Down-the-line return and approach

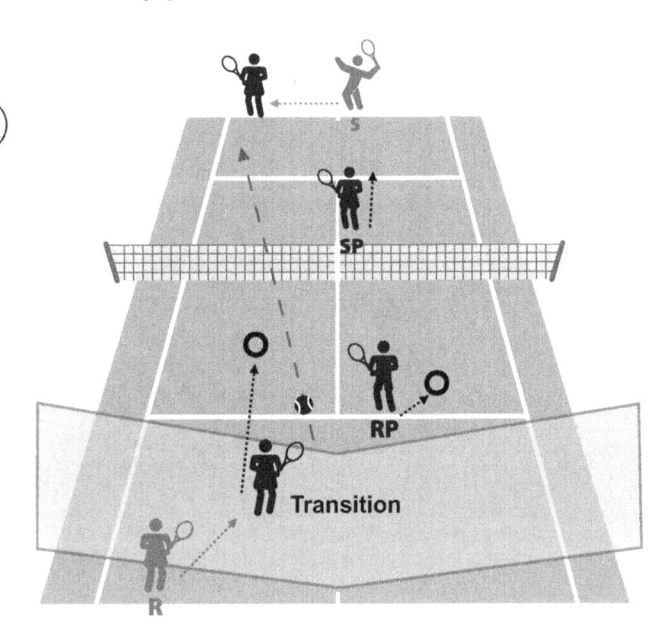

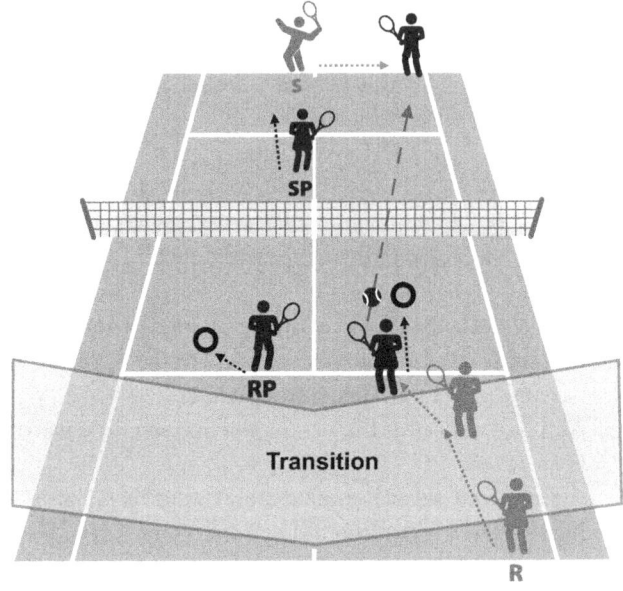

4.2.11 When faced with a team playing Australian formation, approaching on the return will not allow them to move into the playing-straight formation they're attempting to set up. Remember that you'll need to hit your return from well inside the transition zone to make it to your Terminator home in time.

4.2.12 The chip-and-charge variation may be an option on a second serve return. Since you move in before the Server strikes the ball, you're much closer to your Terminator home when you hit your return. Be careful not to hit this ball long, as you have less space when hitting from close to the net and in a down-the-line direction.

4.3 The Workhorse

The Workhorse is the player diagonal to the ball. You become the Workhorse after you hit a crosscourt approach shot and move into the offense zone. You'll remain in this role as long as the point continues in a crosscourt direction.

The Workhorse gets its name from the fact that you'll have to do a lot of running. You'll hit most of the balls, and you're responsible for covering the majority of the court. Your job is to keep the ball in play, while setting up your Terminator partner to finish the point.

As the Workhorse, you'll use your entire arsenal of shots, such as the volley, half-volley, swinging volley, overhead and skyhook.* Make every effort to reach a deep lob before it bounces so your team can maintain its position in the offense zone.

Specific responsibilities include covering:
- all the crosscourt balls, including the short angle;
- middle balls that the Terminator doesn't hit;
- short lobs on your own side;
- all deep lobs, including those over the Terminator.

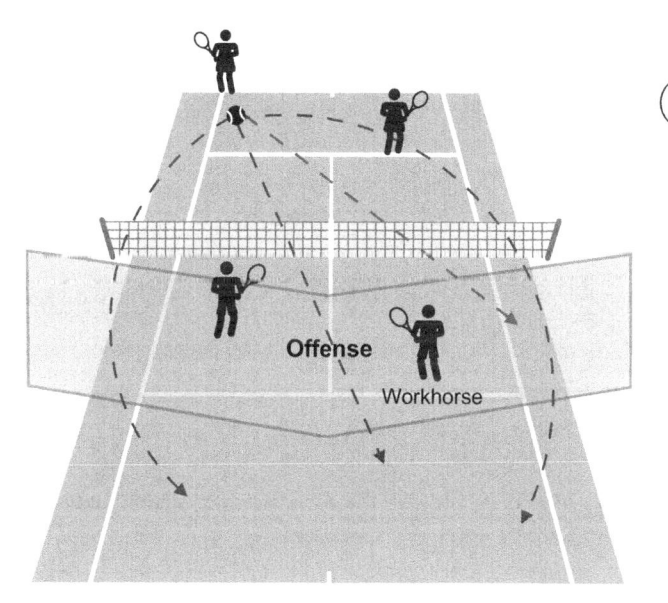

---

*The skyhook is a high forehand volley hit from behind your body. It's used to reach a lob that's too deep to hit with an overhead. By using the skyhook, you can cover many lobs on the forehand side without losing the offensive position.

4.3.1 When playing Workhorse, your usual home is one to two steps in from the service line and equal distance from the center line and singles sideline. You can cover the majority of the court from this location.

The Workhorse | Distance from service line

The average distance for the Workhorse home is one to two steps inside the service line. As Workhorse, be open-minded about varying the distance of your home from the service line depending on your capabilities and your opponents' actions.

As Workhorse, play closer to the net:
- when the opponents never or rarely lob;
- if it looks like your opponent will hit a short-angle crosscourt;
- when you're on the ad side, as the lob over the Terminator is easier to cover with the forehand;
- if you're exceptionally tall or agile;
- in higher level teams.

As Workhorse, play on the service line or slightly behind:
- when the opponents are winning points with successful lobs;
- when you're on the deuce side, as the lob over the Terminator is more difficult to cover with the backhand;
- if you're short and have difficulty reaching lobs;
- if your mobility is limited;
- in lower level teams.

When you're faced with a team that's lobbing really well, both Workhorse and Terminator can move back while still maintaining a stagger.

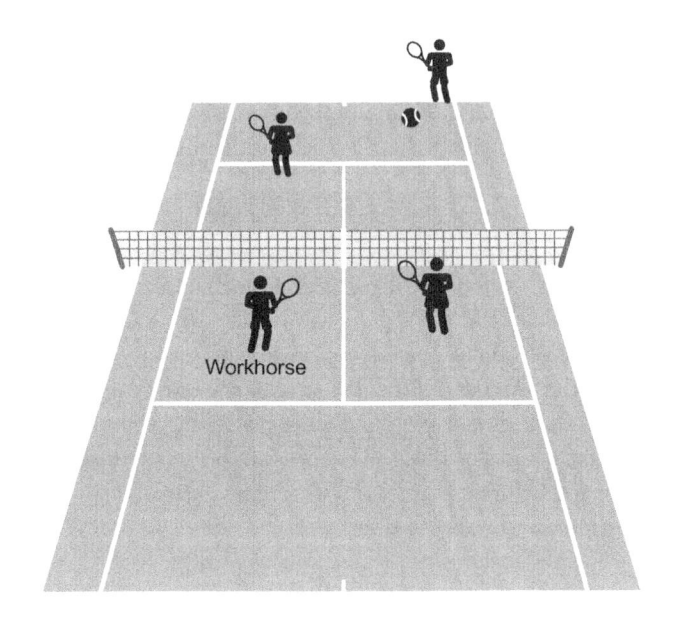

4.3.2 In higher level teams, the Workhorse will probably play closer to the net than the average. You must be agile and alert to cover deep lobs from this location. Maintain some stagger so that the roles remain clear.

The Workhorse | Lateral positioning

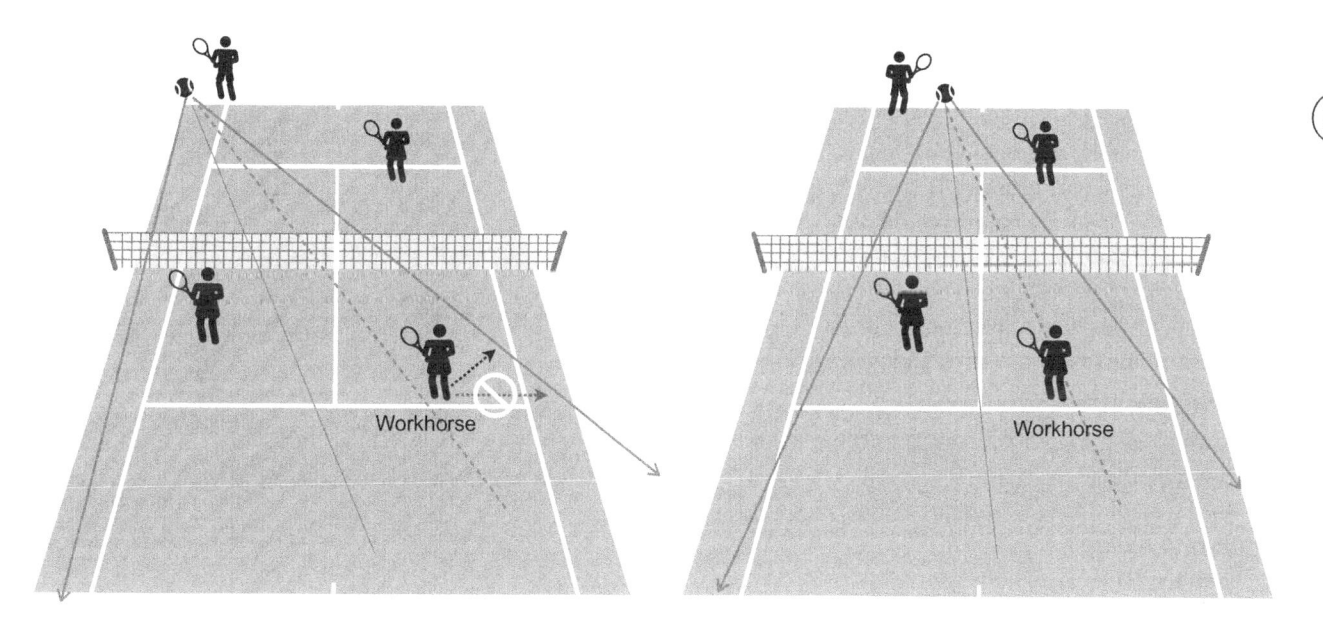

4.3.3 As Workhorse, your usual home is an equal distance from the center line and the singles sideline. When the ball is out wide in the opponents' court, favor covering the angled crosscourt shot by making your home a step toward the singles sideline. To cover an angled shot, move diagonally forward to cut off the angle, thereby shortening the distance to reach the ball.

4.3.4 When the ball in the opponents' court is closer to the middle, favor covering the middle ball by making your home a step toward the center line. The lateral distance between you and your Terminator partner will be closer or farther depending upon where the ball is in the opponent's court. Note that this is different than "the wall" method of positioning, whereby partners try to always maintain the same lateral distance from each other (see diagram 4.1.3).

The Workhorse | Targets

Patience and consistency are key Workhorse attributes. Your job is to keep the ball in play and set your partner up for a winner.

Against a one-up and one-back team, your go-to target is the deep-crosscourt triangle. This shot keeps the ball away from the opposing net player and puts pressure on the baseline player to increase the chance of setting up your partner.

Don't become glued to your home. Be ready to move from your home in any direction and make an effort to move forward to hit a low ball before it bounces.

When playing Workhorse, you must hit up on the ball to get it over the net.

- Hitting up on the ball is a state of mind as well as a physical action.
- From the Workhorse home you're not close enough to the net to hit down to make a winner.
- On a low ball, open your racquet face, bend your knees and get your body down low.
- On a mid-range ball, think about hitting through the ball, facing your racquet in the direction of your target.
- On a high ball, you'll be tempted to hit down. You're still too far away from the net. Think about aiming deep crosscourt.

4.3.5 Train yourself to play the correct shot. As Workhorse, after you hit a ball into the net, notice if you had forgotten your crosscourt target and were thinking about hitting down on the ball. Imagine how it would have felt to have hit up. Visualize where the ball would have landed, shown here as the faint ball in the deep-crosscourt triangle.

The Workhorse | Refined targets

The general target for the Workhorse first and subsequent volleys is the deep-crosscourt triangle. As you gain consistency and experience playing the Workhorse, begin to practice specific targets for the inside and outside ball.* These refined targets are particularly important on your first volley when you're most vulnerable.

Aim outside balls toward the alley.
- The outside ball crosses close to the opposing net player, making the ball placed toward the alley the safest shot.
- There's plenty of angle available to hit toward the alley when hitting the outside ball.

Aim inside balls closer to the middle.
- The inside ball is more difficult for opposing net player to intercept, making the ball placed closer to the middle a safe shot.
- Depending on where the net player is standing, you may be able to aim this ball toward the T.
- The inside ball is liable to land out if it's hit toward the alley.

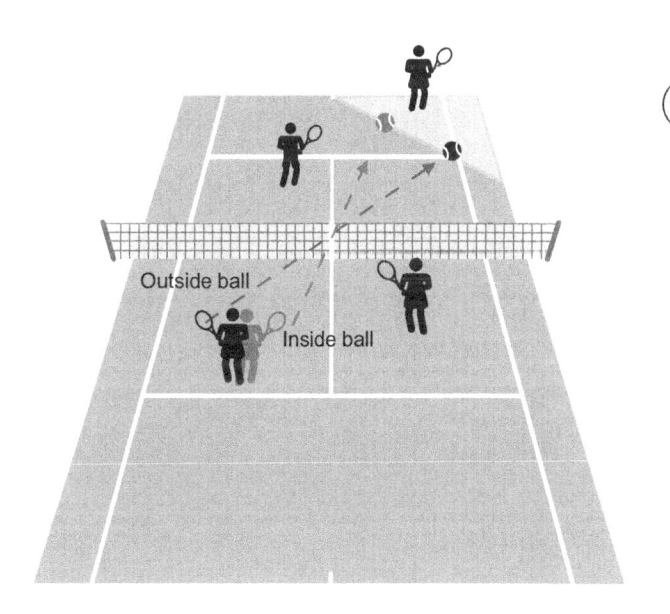

---

* See Blaskower (2007, pages 50-55) for further elaboration of these refined volley targets.

4.3.6 The drill situation is the ideal time to become familiar with these refined targets as you have the opportunity to repeat the same shot many more times than you would in a match. Use the drills in section 5.4 to practice these targets. You can easily remember these targets by thinking "hit the inside ball to the inside (of the court) and the outside ball to the outside."

The Workhorse | Dealing with a short ball

4.3.7a When as Workhorse you're faced with a short floating ball, move quickly toward the attack zone. Now you're close enough to the net to hit down on the ball. Your correct target is down the alley or at the feet of the opposing net player.

4.3.7b The ball's change of direction from crosscourt to down the line means your role changes. You become the Terminator, as you're now directly across from the ball. Your partner moves back from the Terminator home and becomes the Workhorse as she's now diagonal to the ball.

The Workhorse | What not to do with a short ball

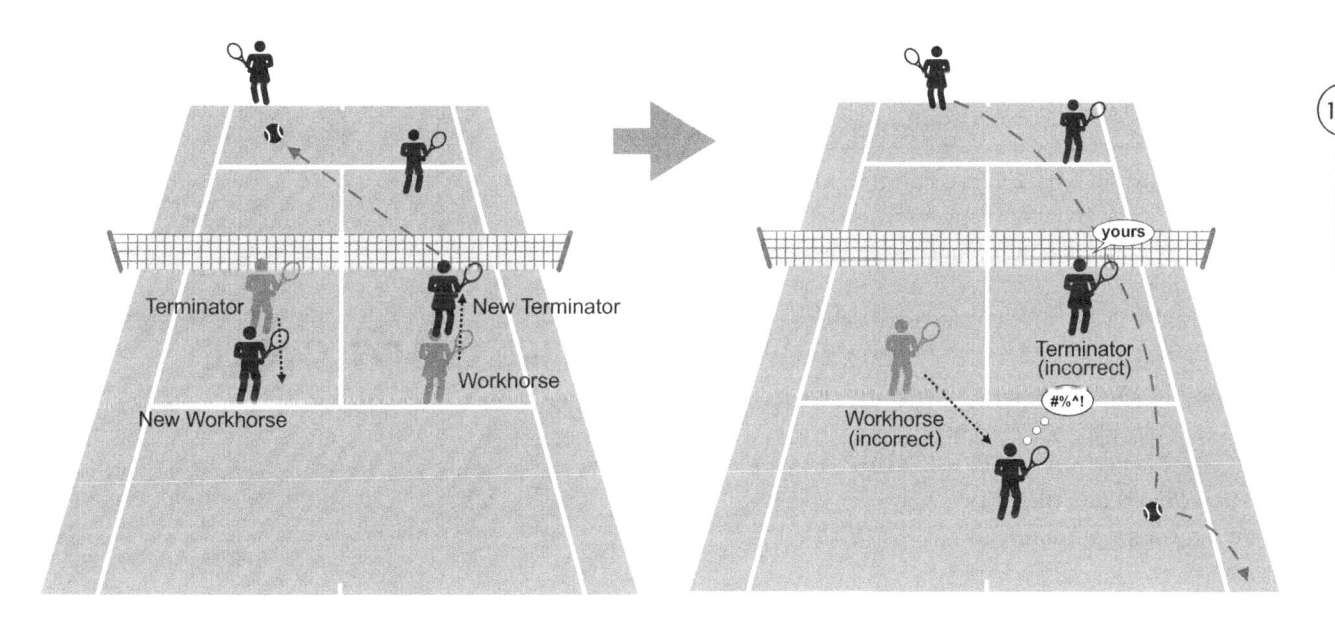

4.3.8a You'll put your team in a precarious situation, called a "reverse stagger," if you move forward and hit the short floating ball crosscourt instead of down the line. Your team is staggered, but you're both in the wrong locations. As the new Terminator, you're diagonal to the ball and the new Workhorse is across from the ball.

4.3.8b The opposing baseline player has plenty of space to hit a crosscourt lob. Even though your team is staggered, your partner will have a hard time chasing down the lob because it's traveling away from her. To avoid this situation, follow this rule: When as Workhorse, you move in and close the net, never hit crosscourt.

The Workhorse | Key points

Centering Moment
- Your Workhorse home is always diagonal to and behind the Terminator.
- Start with your home a step in from the service line. Adjust forward or back depending on your capabilities and what your opponents are doing.
- Center yourself every time your opponent hits the ball and be mentally ready to move in any direction, including backward or diagonally backward to cover a lob.

Receiving Phase
- You're responsible for covering most of the court when you're playing Workhorse.
- Be ready to take the middle ball if needed.
- Hit volleys before the bounce whenever possible, recognizing that some balls are best taken as a half-volley.
- Attempt to reach deep lobs before the bounce.

Sending Phase
- Your primary job is to set up your partner.
- Your go-to target is the deep-crosscourt triangle.
- Lift the ball up to clear the net.
- Recover to you Workhorse home after every crosscourt shot.
- On a short ball that you can hit from near the attack zone, aim straight at the opponent's feet or the down the alley and recover to the Terminator home.

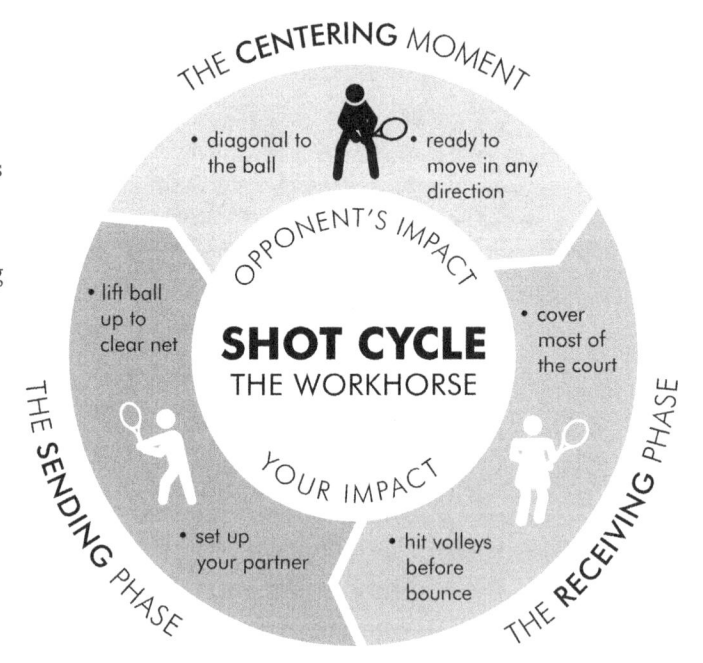

SHOT CYCLE — THE WORKHORSE

- THE CENTERING MOMENT: diagonal to the ball; ready to move in any direction
- OPPONENT'S IMPACT
- THE RECEIVING PHASE: cover most of the court; hit volleys before bounce
- YOUR IMPACT
- THE SENDING PHASE: set up your partner; lift ball up to clear net

4.4 The Terminator

The Terminator is the player directly across from the ball. This means that you're in the same vertical half of the court as the ball. Your role shifts from net player to Terminator after your partner moves into the offense zone. Now that your partner has closed the gap that's a big liability in the one-up and one-back formation, you'll have greater opportunity to do your job of bringing the point to an end (terminating) with a winning volley or overhead.

As Terminator, you're responsible for all drives hit into your half of the court, including balls hit the down the alley, down-the-middle balls that can be poached, and short lobs.

Your role as Terminator has similarities to the net player in the one-up and one-back formation, but the play is much faster because you're both hitting the ball before the bounce. As in one up and one back, your usual home is in the middle of the service box.

Playing Terminator, you'll no longer use the defense-in-offense method (see diagrams 3.2.11–3.2.18), that is backing up when the ball is behind you, because your partner has closed the gap and can cover middle balls. Focus on the play in front of you and be ready to pounce on any opportunity, trusting that your partner will cover anything behind you.

4.4.1 It takes considerable courage to stay up and play from the correct home, especially if you're used to backing up because you have previously played using the wall method. Rest assured, the exhilaration of terminating the point from close to the net is well worth the effort of learning something new.

The Terminator | Distance from net

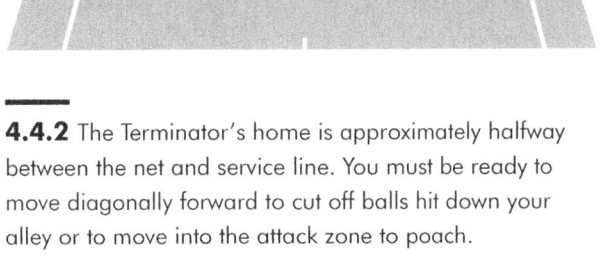

4.4.2 The Terminator's home is approximately halfway between the net and service line. You must be ready to move diagonally forward to cut off balls hit down your alley or to move into the attack zone to poach.

4.4.3 Both members of your team might decide to move back a few steps when faced with opponents who are hitting a lot of difficult lobs. In this case, the Terminator still needs to be ready to move forward to poach or to cover the alley.

The Terminator | Lateral positioning

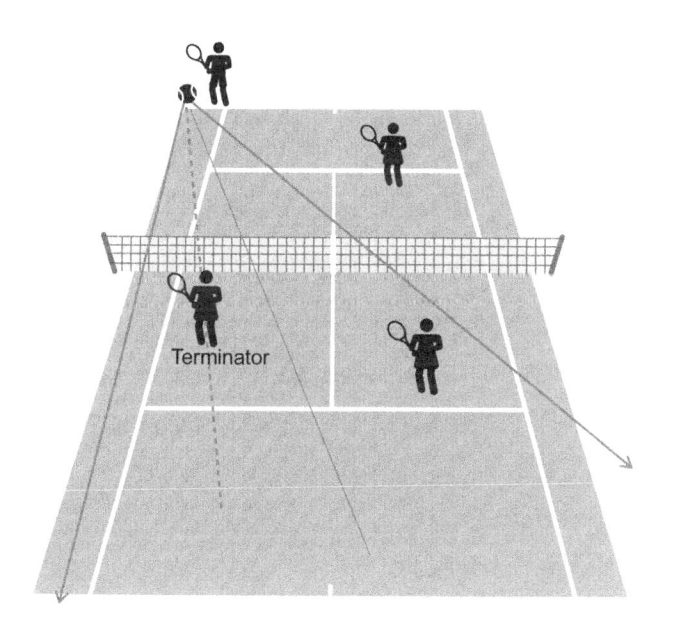

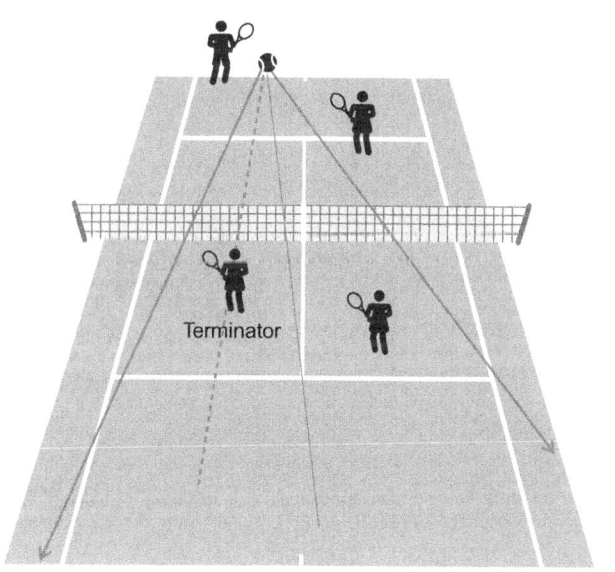

4.4.4 When you're the Terminator and your opponent is hitting from the doubles sideline or wider, move a step toward the singles sideline to adjust to the different angles that are available. Notice how, when you're covering an angled ball, you and your partner's lateral distance from each other is farther apart.

4.4.5 When your opponent is hitting from the inside of her court, take a step toward the center line to adjust to the different angles. Stay alert to the possibility that she might hit down your alley. Notice how, when you're covering a middle ball, you and your partner's lateral distance from each other is closer together.

The Terminator | Targets

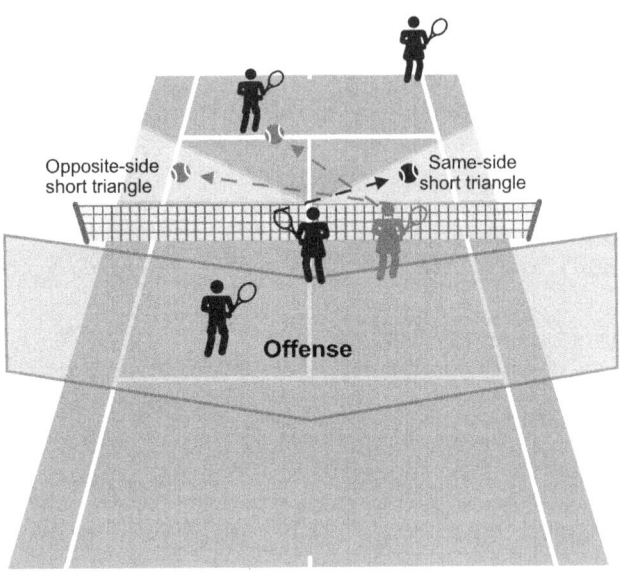

4.4.6 When playing Terminator, move into the attack zone on an appropriate ball and attempt to put the ball away into the diamond-shaped gap between opponents. After hitting the ball, move back to your home in the offense zone.

4.4.7 You'll need to find other targets if the opposing net player is covering the middle. Pay attention to where the openings are and hit into them. When you can hit from within the the attack zone, you're close enough to the net to hit into the short triangles. Sometimes hitting at the opposite net player's feet is the best shot.

The Terminator | Get out of trouble

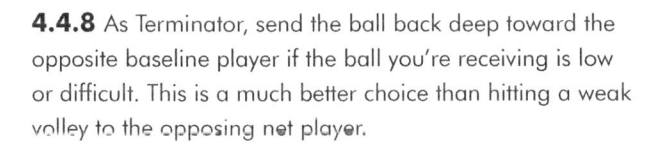

4.4.8 As Terminator, send the ball back deep toward the opposite baseline player if the ball you're receiving is low or difficult. This is a much better choice than hitting a weak volley to the opposing net player.

4.4.9 Play from the correct home to keep you out of trouble. When you move too far back, it's hard to put a ball away, you're more vulnerable to being passed down the alley, and it's confusing for your partner.

The Terminator | Key points

Centering Moment
- Have the courage to play from your correct home halfway between the net and service line.
- Center yourself every time the opponent hits the ball, ready for an opportunity to cut off a ball traveling through the middle of the court.
- Focus your attention in front, and trust your partner to look after the balls that go behind you.

Receiving Phase
- You have a very short amount of time to decide whether or not you'll hit the ball.
- Once you decide whether you'll use a forehand or backhand volley, get turned.
- When receiving a lob, don't move farther back than two or three steps. Let your partner cover the deeper lobs.

Sending Phase
- Whenever possible, move into the attack zone to hit your volley. This allows you to hit down on the ball and opens up more target possibilities.
- Recover to your home after you hit.
- Keep your volleys short and sharp.
- On difficult balls or balls hit straight at you, deflect the volley straight back toward the baseline player in front of you.

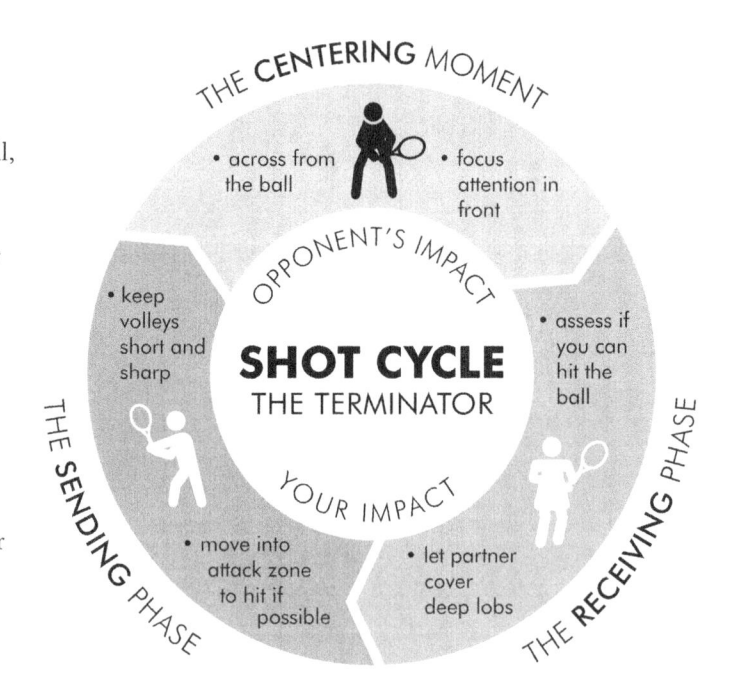

SHOT CYCLE — THE TERMINATOR

THE CENTERING MOMENT
- across from the ball
- focus attention in front

OPPONENT'S IMPACT

THE RECEIVING PHASE
- assess if you can hit the ball
- let partner cover deep lobs

YOUR IMPACT

THE SENDING PHASE
- move into attack zone to hit if possible
- keep volleys short and sharp

4.5 The Dogfight

Dogfight* is when all four players play from inside the offense zone. This is a peak moment because the play is fast and requires utmost focus.

Dogfight happens when:
- the Server and Receiver both approach the net;
- a both-up team is playing a one-up and one-back team, and the baseline player is drawn in;
- both teams love to play both up and will do anything they can to get into the net.

By definition, "dogfight" means "a ferocious struggle for supremacy between interested parties" (New Oxford American Dictionary). To win the struggle, meaning the point, it's crucial to have the daring to play close to the net. Often, one player or team will retreat back to the service line or farther. This team almost always loses the point.

In dogfight, you're susceptible to being lobbed over with a lob volley. However, unless you're getting regularly beaten by the lob, you're better off staying close to the net. Don't try to maintain a staggered formation. The play is too fast to make the adjustments to maintain the Workhorse and Terminator positions.

4.5.1 When a serve and volley is countered with a return and approach, a dogfight ensues.

---

* I learned this name from my longtime doubles partner Anne Marie Vick. I like to use it because it reminds players to be fierce and hold their ground when playing all four up.

The Dogfight | How to win

The team that gets closest to the net usually wins the dogfight and the winning volley is often hit from inside the attack zone. However, you have to earn your right to play from close to the net.

Each time you or your partner hit a volley, you both have enough time to take one step forward or back. If you have sent a low ball, take a step toward the net. If you have sent a high ball, move a step or two back and prepare to defend as your opponent strikes the ball.

A comfortable home is just back from halfway between the net and the service line. You may be forward or back from this location depending on the ball that you have just sent to your opponents.

To win the point:
- Keep the ball low.
- Hit down the middle, between your opponents.
- Hit at your opponent's body at about waist height.
- If one player has weaker volleys, hit to her.
- If one player is retreating back, hit to her feet or into the space that opens up between your two opponents.

4.5.2 When all four players are up at net, hold your ground, stay calm and enjoy. Both partners should be ready and split step every time the opponent hits the ball. Make extra effort to have your racquet in front and keep your center of gravity low.

The Dogfight | Further thoughts

4.5.3 Often a dogfight is created during the middle of a point. If you're at the baseline against a both-up team and your partner is still at net, you may have an opportunity to safely move in if your opponent hits a short volley. Be sure that you're in the offense zone when you hit the ball and hit your approach shot low over the net.

4.5.4 It takes daring to hold your ground at net during the fast exchange of a dogfight. Go for it! Backing up (or never fully moving in) puts you in a poor position to hit strong volleys and opens up a gap between you and your partner.

4.6 Covering the Lob

The staggered-offense system provides clear guidance on whose job it is to cover lobs when playing both up. At its best, it's like a dance when both partners know the moves.

Covering lobs in the both-up formation follows a similar pattern and uses the same method of communication as covering lobs in the one-up and one-back formation (section 3.4). However, it's more challenging because, as Workhorse, you have much less time to respond from your home in the offense zone.

The Terminator takes any lob she can reach without having to move back more than two or three steps. All other lobs, including crosscourt lobs and lobs over the Terminator, belong to the Workhorse. One exception is deep lobs that will land in the alley. Sometimes the Terminator will have a better chance to reach this difficult ball (see diagrams 4.6.6 and 4.6.7).

As Workhorse, make every effort to hit the lob before the bounce so that your team can maintain your both up position in the offense zone. If you don't reach the lob before the bounce, run back to hit it after the bounce and recover to your nearest baseline home. In this case, your partner should move back to the service line or baseline to help in defense. If you're regularly unable to reach the lobs, adjust your Workhorse home farther back.

4.6.1 One of the advantages of the staggered-offense system is that the Workhorse can cover the crosscourt lobs. Remember that from this location you're too far back to hit down on the ball. Hit your overhead more like a serve, hitting up on the ball, or use a skyhook if the ball is behind you. Keep your target crosscourt, deep if possible, and don't expect to hit a winner.

Covering the Lob | Over the terminator

4.6.2 On a short lob, as Terminator, call "mine," and hit the overhead. Aim between your opponents or, if you're well set up and sure you can make a winner, at the opposite net player's feet. If it turns out that the lob is deeper than expected, hit straight back to the baseline player. Recover to your Terminator home as long as the ball is directly across from you.

4.6.3 When the lob travels over the Terminator and down the middle, the Workhorse takes it. There's no need to switch sides. As Workhorse, command, "Got it, stay." Hit the ball before the bounce with an overhead or skyhook, and recover back to your Workhorse home.

Covering the Lob | Before the bounce

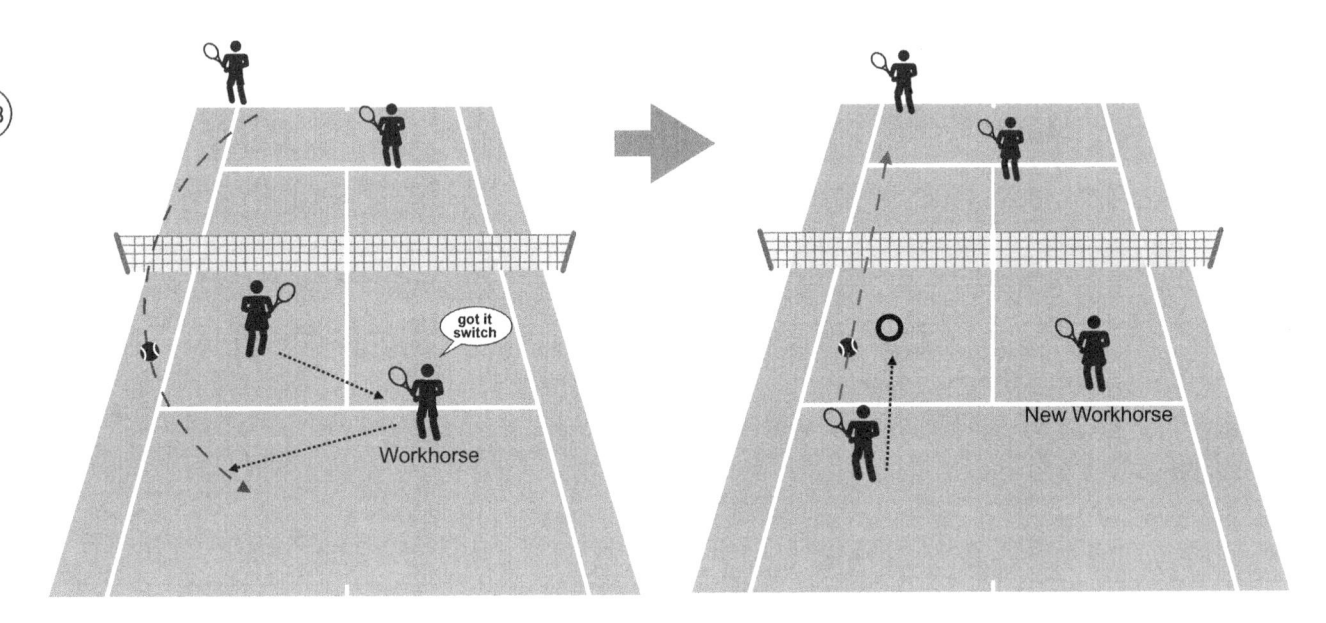

4.6.4a If the lob travels more than two or three steps behind the Terminator, the Workhorse crosses to cover it, promptly communicating, "Got it, switch." The Terminator quickly switches back toward the opposite service line.

4.6.4b If you can hit the ball before it bounces, aim down the line and move in to the Terminator home. Your partner, having switched back, is now the Workhorse. The new Workhorse should be on the lookout for the crosscourt lob on the shot immediately after the switch.

Covering the Lob | After the bounce

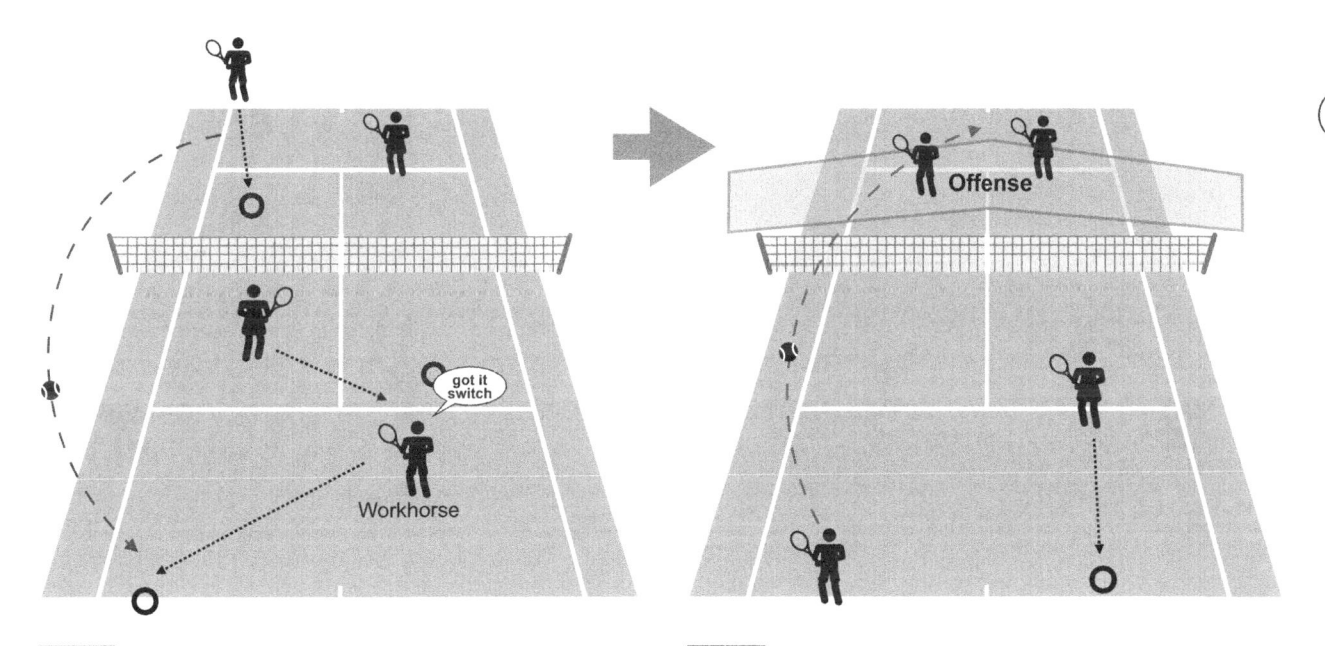

4.6.5a When as Workhorse you can't reach the ball before the bounce, run diagonally back toward the baseline, attempting to get behind the ball to hit it after the bounce. The ideal target is down the line and your recovery is to the baseline home.

4.6.5b Savvy opponents will use this opportunity to move into their offense zone. If the lob you're receiving is very difficult, or if the opponent approaches the net, the safest choice is to hit a high lob. In this case your partner should move back to the baseline to help you defend.

Covering the Lob | Down-the-alley lob

4.6.6 Sometimes the Terminator can reach a down-the-alley lob that the Workhorse can't. For example, as Terminator, you might go for this deep shot that's in your ad-side alley, if you know that your partner has difficulty moving to the left to reach lobs on her backhand side. Communication is essential as this is an exception to the Terminator's usual range of responsibility. Once you've called for the ball, don't back out. Do everything you can to reach it.

4.6.7 In a lefty-righty team, as the right-handed Terminator, you can use your forehand to cover a down-the-alley lob on the deuce side that your left-handed partner would need to reach with her backhand. The same thinking applies on the ad side when a lefty Terminator can cover the alley lob on the ad side with her forehand. Try to reach the ball before it bounces and aim your shot down the line. Recover to your Terminator home.

4.7 Both Up Against Both Back

A team playing both back in the defense zone can retrieve many balls. In fact, a both-back team can be more difficult to play against than a one-up and one-back team, as you have no obvious target or space to put the ball away between the opponents.

At this point you, as the both-up team, have to completely change your game plan. First and foremost, be patient. It may take a few shots before you can hit a short-angle shot or a drop-shot for a winner.

Hit all balls, both overheads and volleys, straight in front of you and within the singles lines. This will take away your opponents' angles. Pay careful attention to your Workhorse and Terminator roles as they'll frequently change. Remember that you're the Terminator whenever you hit straight in front of you.

Make every effort to reach all lobs before the bounce so that your team can maintain its position in the offense zone.

Wait for your opponent to hit a weak or slightly higher ball before going for a winner. Then move into the attack zone and hit into a short triangle with an angled volley or drop shot. On a short lob, you may be able to finish the point with a short-angled overhead.

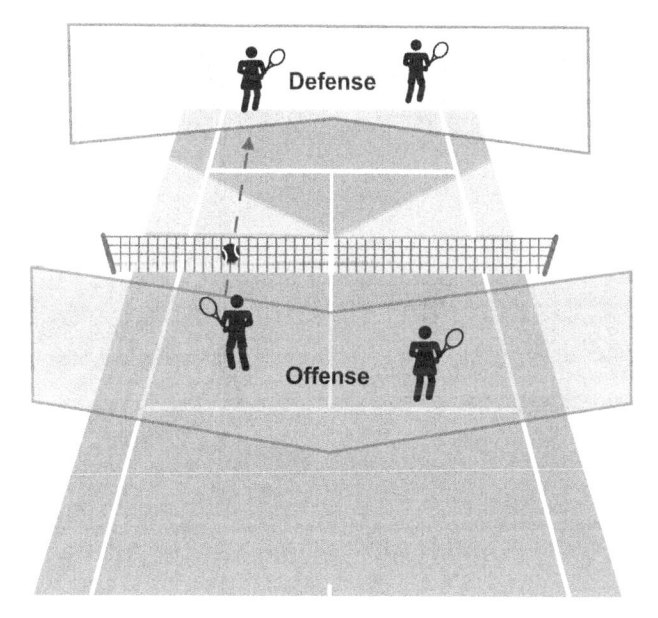

4.7.1 "You have been beating them with your crosscourt game; now you'll have to beat them with your straight game." — Helle Sparre (personal communication, 2011)

Both Up Against Both Back | Play the straight game

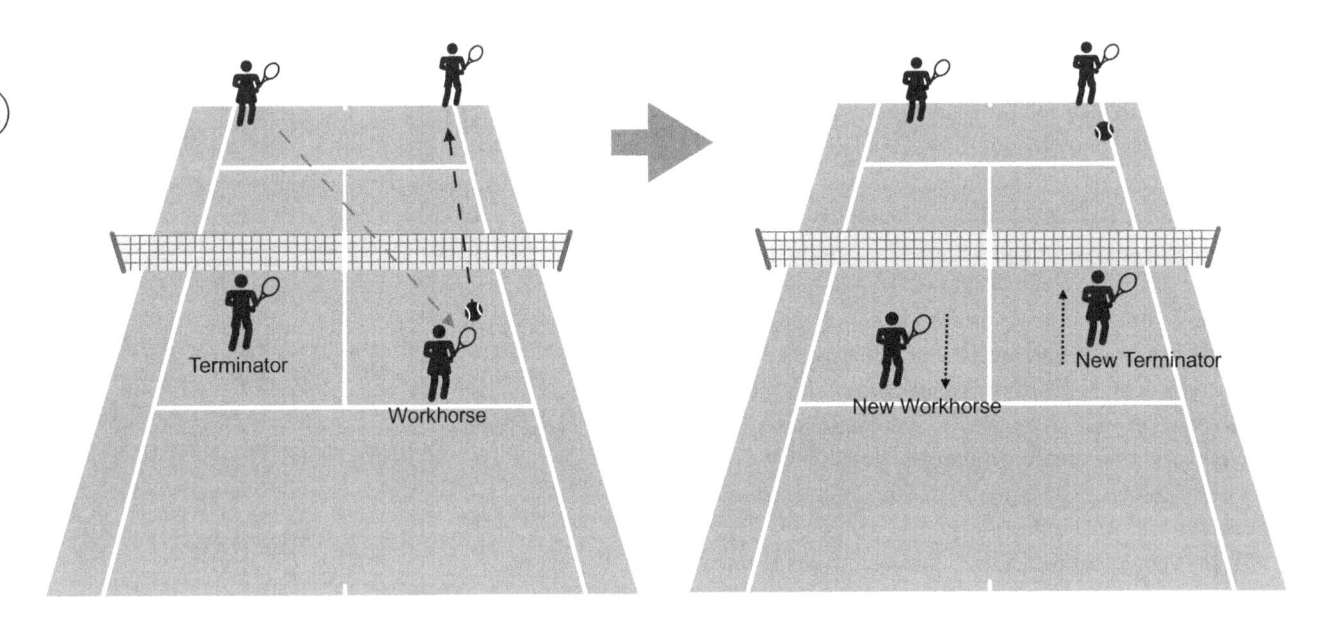

4.7.2a As Workhorse, you have redirected the crosscourt ball by hitting straight in front of you. Hitting straight in front of you takes away your opponents' angles.

4.7.2b Now the ball is directly in front of you and you move forward into the Terminator home. Your partner, now diagonal to the ball, moves back to the Workhorse home.

4.8 Both Back

When you move into a both-back formation to defend from the defense zone, you're no longer split between two zones.

Many players shy away from moving back because they feel like they're giving up. They've been taught to "rush and crush" without learning that sometimes it's better to defend. It takes a shift in perspective to realize that, once your opponents have filled the offense zone, you're actually in a better position to win the point if you join your partner in the defense zone.

Always let the ball bounce when playing from the defense zone. Take your time. Your goal is to take control of the point by varying the pace, spin and height of your shots. Your tools are lobs, drives and the short-angle crosscourt. When hitting drives, keep the ball low.

- Move your opponents forward and back.
- Run down every ball and be ready to run for a short ball.
- Force your opponents to make an error or weak volley.
- Use the short-angle crosscourt when you're hitting a shorter ball from inside the transition zone.
- If you or your partner hit a lob that your opponents can't hit before the bounce, both move in and take over the offense zone.

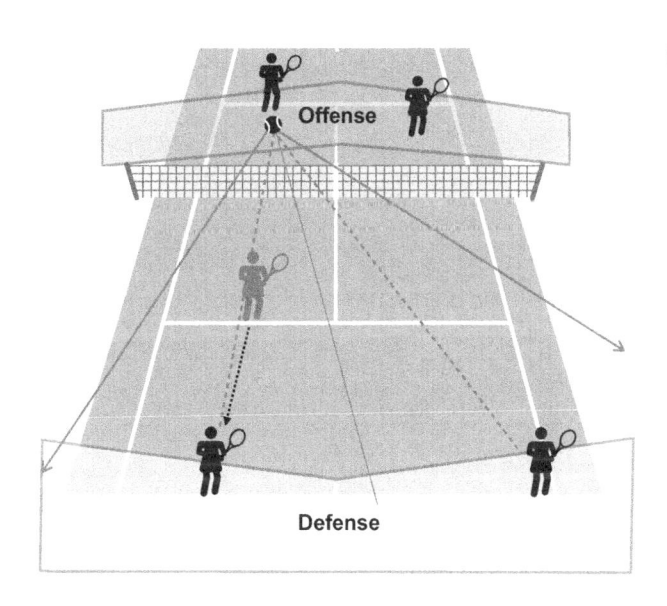

4.8.1 Notice the location of the homes of the players in the defense zone. The player diagonal to the ball (on deuce side) positions herself near the singles sideline. The player across from the ball (on ad side) positions herself on the baseline, halfway between the doubles sideline and center mark. Both players are on the baseline, ready to sprint forward or move back, depending on the ball that is sent.

Both Back | The perils of not moving back

4.8.2 Your partner, the net player in the near court, is leaving it up to you to face the opposing team from the baseline. Using the "pick and stick" tactic (see diagram 4.1.10), the far-court Workhorse picks on you, consistently hitting deep crosscourt volleys until the Terminator is able to cut off a ball and stick it to your partner.

4.8.3 Tired of facing the offensive team on your own, you try to join your partner in the offense zone. You only manage to get a few steps into the transition zone before the diagonal net player volleys directly at you. From your poor position, you make a weak reply that the opposing net player puts away.

Both Back | How to get into both back

The decision to play both back is often made during the middle of a point as a response to your opponents moving into a both-up formation.

After your opponents have filled the offense zone, it's your responsibility as the net player to get from the offense zone back to the baseline to help your partner defend. It takes some finesse to get there without getting caught in the transition zone. Your opponents' shots are coming back fast as they're now hitting before the bounce and from a location close to the net. You need to find a way to get all the way back to the baseline in between your opponents' hits without getting caught in the transition zone.

You might think of this as a reverse approach shot, although it's your partner who's hitting the ball while you move. If she can hit a lob off the opponent's approach shot, you may have enough time to reach your home on the baseline.

Oftentimes your partner won't be able to hit a lob without putting you at risk. If she doesn't lob, move back to the service line and get ready to defend from there. You'll need to wait for the next shot to get back to the baseline.

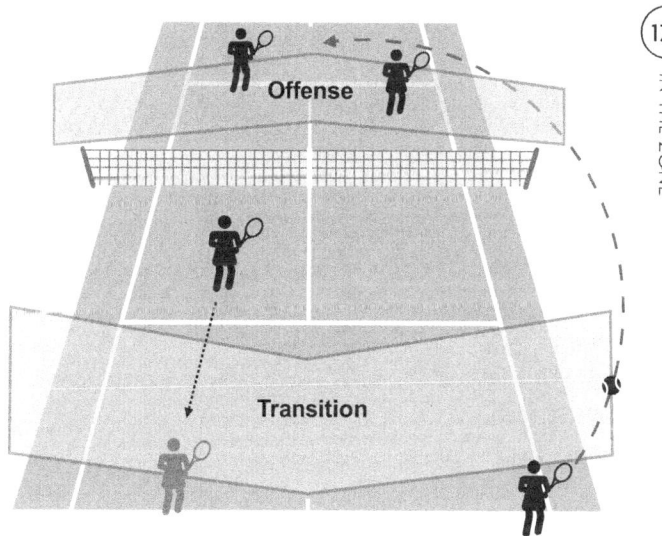

4.8.4 Immediately move back to the baseline if your partner hits a lob off the opponent's approach shot. Remember to be centered and ready when the opponent strikes the ball, even if you don't make it all the way to your baseline home.

Both Back | Get back in two parts

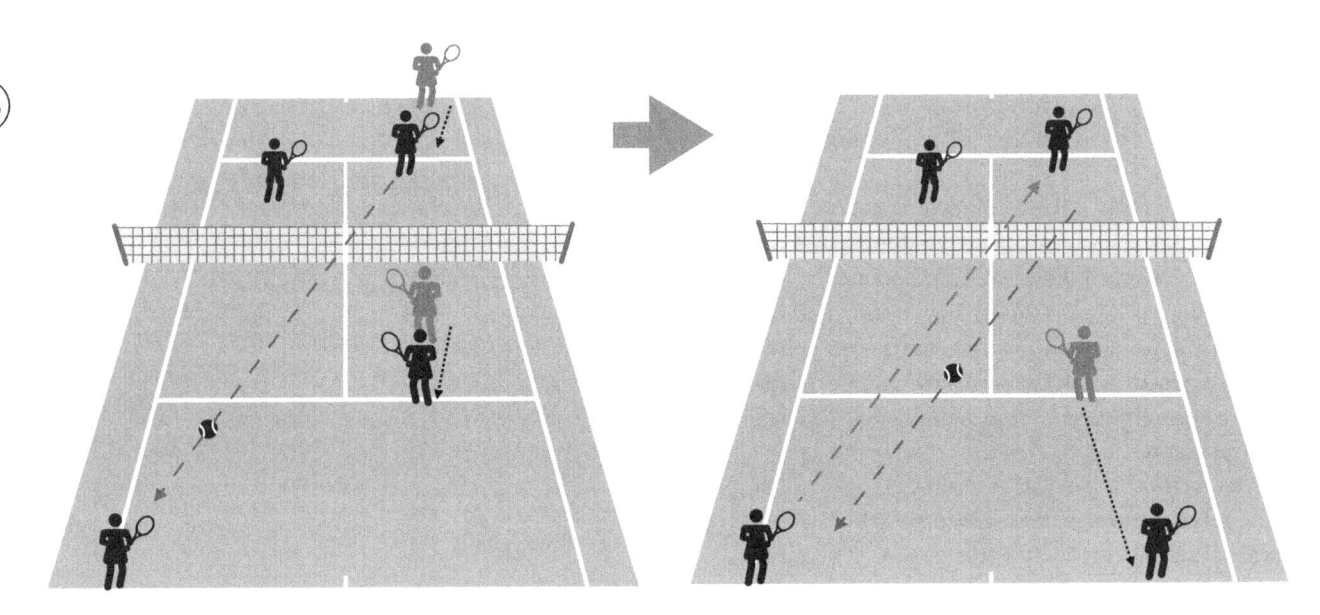

4.8.5a If your partner doesn't hit a lob to give you time to move back, you'll need to move back in two parts. First, once your opponents have filled the offense zone, move back to the service line as soon as the ball is behind you and before your partner hits the ball.

4.8.5b Next, if your partner manages to keep the ball in play and you don't get nailed in the meantime, scoot back to the baseline the very next time the ball is behind you.

Both Back | Defense tools

Move your opponents up and back when playing from the defense zone. Notice where your opponents are positioned and look for the spaces between them.

Tool #1: Lobs
- Hit down-the-line or over-the-middle lobs. Against a team playing staggered offense, the crosscourt lob is less effective because the Workhorse is farther back.
- Height is more important than depth. Make your opponents move and reach.
- Don't expect to hit winning lobs. Just hit deep enough to force your opponent to hit her overhead from behind the service line.
- If either opponent has to run back and let your lob bounce, you have won back the offense territory and both you and your partner can move in.

Tool #2: Drives
- Hit hard flat drives down the middle that travel low over the net. Keeping the ball low prevents your opponents from putting the ball away and forces them to hit up.
- Aim crosscourt topspin dipping shots to drop at the farther opponent's feet.

Tool #3: Short-angle crosscourt
- Wait until hitting from the transition zone before trying this lower percentage shot.

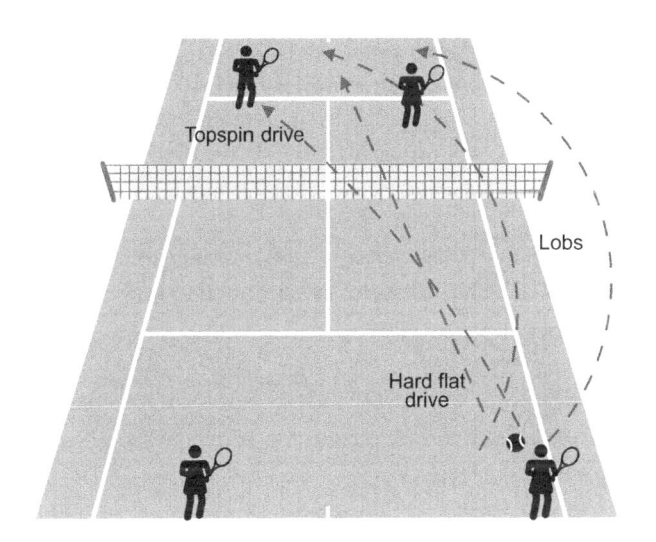

4.8.6 When playing from the defense zone, trust that you have plenty of time. Don't be in a rush to win the point. Be prepared to run down every ball, always let the ball bounce, and use a variety of lobs and drives so you don't become predictable. Keep recovering back to your home in the defense zone and be ready to move forward if either opponent hits a short ball.

Both Back | Against the wall

Learn to assess where your opponents are positioned in their offense zone. You have time for a quick glance at them while you're receiving the ball.

If you see your opponents line up side by side in the offense zone, they're using the wall method. Avoid hitting your usual crosscourt drive to the player approaching the net as it will go right into her strike zone.

It may seem like your opponents' advance into the net happens quickly. Stay calm. Pay attention to how they're winning points and figure out what adjustments you need to make.

Tool #1: Lobs
- Lob over the shorter player or over the backhand side of either player.
- Hit a crosscourt lob if the diagonal player has moved in close to the net.
- Lob over the middle, especially if you're playing a lefty-righty team with their backhands in the middle.

Tool #2: Drives
- Hit hard flat or topspin drives down the middle.

Tool #3: Short-angle crosscourt
- Use the short-angle crosscourt on a wide ball when you're hitting from inside the transition zone.

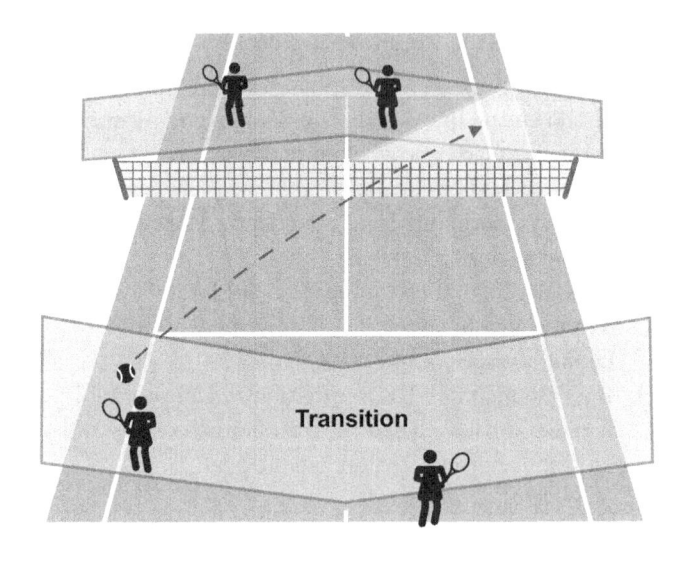

4.8.7 The short-angle crosscourt is a smart choice if you're hitting from inside the transition zone and the opposing team has moved over to cover the possibility of a down-the-alley shot.

Both Back | Against a team hanging back

Sometimes you'll notice your both-up opponents making a wall farther back at the service line. It's difficult for them to put the ball away from there, so they'll keep putting the ball in play and wait for your mistake.

Tool #1: Drives
- Keep your shots out of their strike zones by aiming at their feet, down the middle, or down the alley.

Tool #2: Lobs
- Use the lob to move your opponents back and get them out of position. Don't expect to make a winning lob over their heads. Just make them hit their overheads from a couple of steps behind the service line.
- Hit lobs to their backhand sides or down the middle.

Tool #3: Short-angle crosscourt
- This shot is easier to hit against opponents who hang back as they can't cover as much side-to-side territory.

Pay attention if your partner gets drawn forward on a short ball. When playing against a team hanging back, you have more time to get into the offense zone without getting caught in the transition zone. If you both make it in without mishap, you're in a dogfight. Now keep the ball low and continue to move in.

4.8.8 Don't underestimate a team that hangs back on the service line. They've probably played this way for many years, so expect them to return shots that other players would miss. Be patient and wait for the right opportunity to hit between them, hit a short-angle crosscourt, or both move forward into dogfight.

Both Back | Against the charger

The "charger" sprints forward after her approach, trying to get as close as possible to put away her volley. She's on top of the net before you know it, possibly not even pausing to split step.

The first time this happens, you'll probably be caught unaware. You hit crosscourt into the charger's strike zone and your partner gets pummeled.

Be ready. Only let this happen once!

The challenge is to identify what just happened and immediately change your shot selection. You won't get a second chance if you hit a mid-height crosscourt drive to the charger.

- Hit a crosscourt lob over the charger directly from her approach shot.
- If the charger is reaching your lobs with a strong overhead, lob over her partner.
- If the charger's partner moves back, hit straight toward her, or hit into the space that opens up between the two opponents.
- If the charger's partner stays close to net, follow the advice for defending against the wall formation (see diagram 4.8.7).

4.8.9 Notice that the offensive team in the far end is in a reverse staggered formation (see diagram 4.3.8a.) Whenever you're playing against a both-up team, be on the lookout for the reverse stagger. When you see it, take the opportunity to send a crosscourt lob over the diagonal player's head (see diagram 4.3.8b).

In the Zone | Summary

Playing in the Same Zone
- Staggered offense is a both-up system that can give your team almost complete coverage of the court.
- This system provides clarity about who's responsible for covering deep lobs and middle balls, and for putting the ball away.

The Approach Shot
- The quality of your approach shot (the shot that brings you to net to join your partner) directly affects the likelihood of you winning the point.
- If approaching crosscourt, aim deep, and keep the ball inside the singles lines to take away the opposing baseline player's angles.
- Approaching the net directly from the serve or return will get you into a both-up formation early in the point.

The Workhorse
- The Workhorse is the player diagonal to where the ball is in the opponents' court.
- Work to set up your partner by hitting into the deep-crosscourt triangle and cover all the deep lobs.
- Resist the urge to hit down on the ball or go for winners when playing from the Workhorse home.

The Terminator
- The Terminator is the player directly across from where the ball is in the opponents' court.
- Be aggressive, moving diagonally forward to poach or cover your alley.
- Play from your correct home in the middle of the service box and trust that your partner will back you up.

The Dogfight
- The dogfight is the "ferocious struggle" that occurs when all four players are playing from within the offense zone.
- The team that keeps the ball low and moves in close to the net usually wins the point.

Covering the Lob
- The ability of the Workhorse to cover the deep lobs and provide back-up coverage on a middle ball are strengths of the staggered-offense system.

Both Up Against Both Back
- Hit all balls straight in front until you have the opportunity to move forward and hit a short-angled shot or drop shot for a winner.

Both Back
- As your consistency improves and points get longer, you'll have opportunities to defend together from the defense zone when faced with a both-up team.
- Take your time. There's no rush to end the point and the longer you can keep the ball in play, the more likely it is that your opponents will make a mistake.

(182)

CHAPTER 5

Practice Skills

5.1 Why Practice?

If you want to improve your tennis, practice as well as taking lessons and playing games. Aim to practice at least as often as you play a match. By practice, I mean hitting balls or playing points, outside of social or competitive match play, with specific goals in mind.

You can practice with another player or players, a coach or a ball machine. All are useful. To attain a healthy balance, you'll want to be sure to include some live-ball hitting into your practice routine. A "live" ball is a ball hit back and forth between two or more players. This is opposed to a "dead" ball fed from either a basket or ball machine.

This chapter is filled with ideas for drills and games to play with a hitting partner, without the need of a coach. Most are designed for two or four players hitting live balls with each other. The drills can either be practiced co-operatively, with the aim of lengthening the rally, or competitively, with the goal of winning a point. Include both methods, finding a balance that supports the goals of your practice session.

Hint: Often the method we least like is the one we most need to do.

There are many great reasons to practice:
1. Practice is the time when you can focus on your own strokes, movement and patterns without having to think about how you're going to win the set and match.
2. Practice improves your match play because it gives you dedicated time to work on different aspects of your game.
3. You hit many more balls in practice than when playing games.
4. Practicing without a coach builds self-reliance and confidence.
5. Technical changes must go through a stage of practice before integrating into match play.
6. Practice allows you to become comfortable with new doubles tactics and court movement patterns.
7. Practice gives you an opportunity to develop your strengths and work on your weaknesses.
8. In practice you can explore a wider variety of shots than your norm.
9. Playing out points in a practice setting improves your ability to perform well when it counts.
10. Practice is fun and provides great exercise.

Why Practice? | Ball machine or live ball

Ball-machine Practice

Advantages:
- The *Play Book** drills are doubles specific.
- The ball machine allows for repetition of patterns and shots.
- Practicing longer sequences on the ball machine encourages focus.
- It provides opportunities to return difficult shots.
- It allows freedom to develop power and put the ball away.
- It provides possibilities to learn and practice complicated movement patterns. Even less experienced or less consistent players can benefit.
- Players of different levels can practice together.

Disadvantages:
- You can't see the opposing player's racquet or body position.
- Consistency can easily be ignored.
- The ball is always sent from the same place on the court.
- The balls sent can become too predictable.
- A competitive element is difficult to incorporate.
- You can't practice return of serve with a standard ball machine.
- Your serve must be practiced independently of ball machine practice.

Live-ball Practice

Advantages:
- It's more realistic to hit against a human player than a ball machine.
- The ball is sent from different places on the court.
- You can learn to anticipate by watching the opposing player's movement and racquet.
- Live-ball practice encourages consistency, as a missed ball ends the rally.
- It's easy to incorporate scoring and competition.
- It provides the unpredictability of point play.

Disadvantages:
- Live-ball practice requires considerable self-discipline.
- Different level players may find it less satisfying to practice together.
- It's difficult to set up a repetitive poaching drill in a live-ball situation.
- It's challenging to practice more complicated tactics without a coach.

---

* Valerie Clarke and I have developed a series of doubles drills and a reference called *The Play Book* (2019) for use with PLAYMATE ball machines. Our drills are designed to simulate real doubles situations, so you can practice your doubles shots while learning correct movement patterns. Get access to our drills by requesting theplaybookdrills@gmail.com under the "Friends" tab of the LikeMyDrill app.

Why Practice? | Tips for live-ball practice

Making tactical changes is less jarring to your existing game than making technical ones. Even so, anytime you change an established pattern, there's a period where you have to think a lot about what you're doing. In the beginning, you may feel like you're playing worse. This is where practice and training are essential. Once you have moved to a certain place on the court or hit to a particular target enough times, it becomes natural and effortless.

Plan Your Practice

- Have a goal for your practice, such as increasing consistency from the baseline, integrating a technical change, or improving your play from the Workhorse position.
- Plan which drills you'll practice and for how long, choosing drills that support your goal.
- Keep your practice session moving along, changing drills frequently to keep you fresh and alert.
- Once you know the pattern of a particular drill, keep score to help you to stay focused and bring in a competitive element.
- When drilling, always have a target in mind.
- Don't hit balls you think are going out.
- Spend at least 10 to 15 minutes in the beginning of your session with drills that warm up your body.
- Include racquet-to-racquet volleys, full-court crosscourt hitting, and serve and return practice in every session.
- To integrate the skills you have worked on, conclude your practice with some point play that includes serve and return.
- Unless otherwise stated, always use the doubles sidelines as your outside boundary when you practice.
- One to two hours is an appropriate length for a practice session.

Equipment

- Use new or nearly new balls when practicing. Six balls per two players should be plenty. You'll be rallying back and forth, so it's important that the balls resemble what you'd use in match play. The exception is for serving practice, where it's fine to use a hopper of balls that are more worn.
- If you're a beginner or any time you're working on a new technical skill, begin with half-court drills and play with slower balls, such as foam, orange or green dot balls.
- When you're working on positioning, place round markers on the court to designate the locations of your ideal home.
- When you're working on improving your accuracy, place line markers on the court to create target areas.

Why Practice? | Practice safely

Practicing with four players and two live balls on one court is a great use of court space, especially if court time is limited or costly. However, even as you focus on your own rally, keep in mind that you're sharing the court.

Be especially mindful when practicing crosscourt drills on the full court.

- If the drill involves a net player (diagrams 5.4.1 to 5.4.6), always have both net players on the same end of the court.
- If the drill involves serving and receiving (diagrams 5.5.2 to 5.5.5), the two Servers should be on the same end of the court.
- Go for control and placement rather than power when hitting overheads.
- Keep an eye on stray balls and alert any player who may be in danger of stepping on a ball.

Take extra care when playing two games of ghost doubles simultaneously on one court (diagram 5.6.1). Play a let (take the point over) rather than getting in the way of another player. Wait to serve if either of the players playing points on the other side are at the net. Feel free to take turns if that feels more comfortable.

Finally, remember to take breaks and drink water at regular intervals. You won't have the regular end changes that a match provides.

5.1.1 Practice safely by being aware and respectful of the other players on the court.

5.2 Half-Court Drills

The half-court drills are an efficient way to hit many balls in a short amount of time. They're excellent for warming up and developing technical skills.

Foam, orange or green dot progressive balls are softer and help slow the ball down for beginners, making it easier to lengthen the rally. All levels of players can benefit from using the slower balls from time to time, especially when warming up or making technical changes.

The first three drills use the service line as the end boundary. These drills are recommended for developing volley technique and improving groundstroke and volley control. They're also good for warming up.

The last two drills are fast-paced volley drills which are played from inside the half court but don't use the service line as the end boundary. These are great for developing reflexes and improving quick reaction volleys.

Drills one through four use either the left or the right side of the half court so that you're hitting from a doubles perspective. When your hitting partner is straight in front of you, one player will be on the deuce side and the other on the ad. When hitting crosscourt, you and your hitting partner will be diagonal to each other, either both on the deuce side or both on the ad side. For practice purposes, the center line becomes one of the side boundaries for your shots.

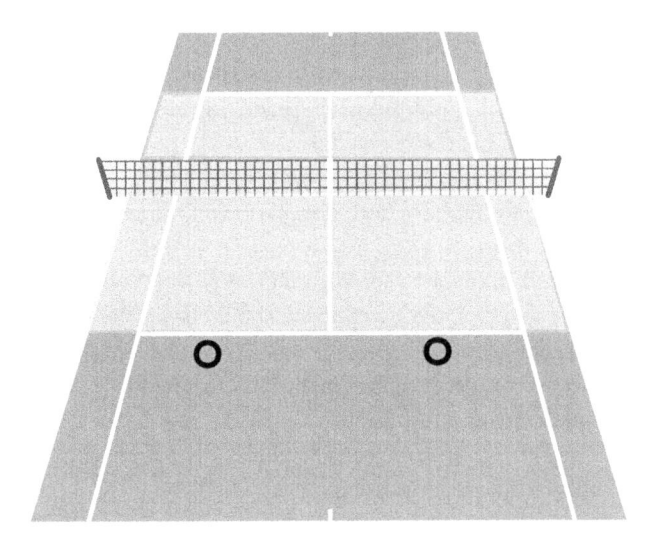

5.2.1 The half court is the area between the service line and the net. It includes the alleys when practicing doubles. When hitting half-court groundstrokes, your home is behind the service line.

Half-Court Drills | Mini-tennis

Develops focus, control and footwork skills on your groundstrokes and volleys.

- For two or four players. If four on court, two live balls will be used at once.
- 10 to 15 minutes.

Mini-tennis is an excellent warm-up activity. Choose a focus, such as moving your feet or watching the ball, to help get your mind settled. Shorten your backswing, but use a full follow-through when hitting mini-tennis groundstrokes.

Directions

If available, place court markers to show where the homes are behind the service line and at net.
1. Hit groundstrokes back and forth for three to five minutes, using the service line as the end boundary.
2. One player moves up to net, halfway between the net and service line. Rally for three to five minutes with the net player hitting soft volleys. Aim your volleys to land about halfway between the net and service line.
3. Change positions. The player on the service line moves to the net and the net player moves back to the service line. Rally for three to five minutes.

Variation: To practice your half-volley, ask the net player to aim his volleys just inside the service line.

5.2.2 Hitting mini-tennis with one player at net (Step 2) is an ideal way for beginners to practice volleys in a live-ball situation, when hitting between the net and baseline is still too difficult. Work co-operatively, controlling your shots so that your rallies get longer.

Half-Court Drills | Crosscourt mini-tennis

Improves consistency and develops your ability to hit volleys with direction.

- For two or four players. If four on court, two live balls will be used at once.
- 18 minutes.

Crosscourt mini-tennis is especially relevant for players who can't yet maintain a consistent crosscourt rally from the baseline. Move back toward the baseline as you improve.

Directions

When hitting crosscourt, turn your body on an angle to face the player you're hitting with. Play from a home behind the service line so you have time to respond to balls that land on or near this end boundary.

1. Hit crosscourt groundstrokes for three minutes, using the service line as the end boundary.
2. One player (or two players if four on court) moves up to net, halfway between the net and service line. Rally crosscourt for three minutes, with the net player hitting volleys.
3. Change positions. The service line player will now be hitting volleys and vice versa. Rally crosscourt for three minutes.
4. Change sides (deuce to ad) and repeat Steps 1, 2 and 3.

5.2.3 The volley-to-groundstroke step is beneficial if you're working on volley technique as the different crosscourt angles take many repetitions before they become automatic. Aim your volleys halfway between the net and service line to develop control and keep the rally going.

Half-Court Drills | Cat and mouse

Develops control, touch and your short-angle crosscourt.

- For two or four players. If four on court, two live balls will be used at once.
- Six to eight minutes.

Cat and Mouse is fun and it develops your short-angle crosscourt that's hit from close to the net. I was first introduced to this drill by Helle Sparre in 2011 when we used it as a warm-up.

Directions

If available, place line markers to delineate the boundary of the short triangles. Start from the outer back corner of the service box.

1. Rally crosscourt groundstrokes for three to four minutes or play the first to seven points.
   - Aim your shots into the short triangle, including the alley.
   - You can use both topspin and slice shots. A backhand slice works particularly well for this shot.
   - This is a groundstroke practice. Let the balls bounce.
   - Occasionally it will make sense to hit a ball as a volley, but don't hit balls you think are going out.
2. Change sides (deuce to ad) and repeat.

5.2.4 Your home for Cat and Mouse is the outer back corner of the service box. If you're a player who prefers to hit forehands, you'll be tempted to stand in the alley to avoid your backhand on the ad side (or deuce side for a lefty). Don't do this as it's not a shot you'd hit when you're playing a point. Practice properly and use your backhand when it's on the outside.

Half-Court Drills | Racquet-to-racquet volleys

Improves your reaction volleys and ability to stay calm under fire.

- For two or four players. If four on court, two live balls will be used at once.
- Three to 10 minutes.

This drill is essential for improving your volleys and should be included for at least a few minutes in every practice. Even beginners will enjoy the challenge and excitement of keeping the rally going without the ball bouncing.

Directions

Rally or play points with the intention of hitting continuous volleys.
- Hit all balls before the bounce as best as you can, moving forward to hit your volleys rather than backing up.
- Include the alleys for improving reach, or exclude them for building control.
- For co-operative, start two or three steps in from the service line and keep count of how many in a row you can hit.
- For competitive, start from the service line and step in on every hit where you keep the ball low. Keep score, playing the first to seven points.

5.2.5 The key to this drill is being aware of your centering moment. If you're calm and centered, with the racquet in the correct ready position every time your hitting partner strikes the ball, you'll find that everything else will fall into place.

Variations: Play crosscourt, hit only forehand or only backhand volleys, or play co-operatively volleying farther back from service line to service line.

Half-Court Drills | Pepper

Encourages fearless net play while developing your reflexes, touch and lob volleys.

- For two players.
- Play for as long as it's fun.

This advanced drill gets its name from a volleyball drill in which two players alternate between a bump, set and spike. In this co-operative tennis drill, two players alternate between a volley, lob volley and overhead. A lob volley is a volley hit with an open racquet face, causing the ball to travel up in the air as a lob.

Give yourself a few minutes to get into the rhythm of Pepper. After awhile you'll be able to hit the overheads with increased power while still maintaining the control you need to keep your hitting partner safe.

Directions

Both players start on the service line. Play from the middle of the court to give you some extra space.

1. Player A (in the near court) starts with an underhand feed, simulating the volley.
2. Player B hits a lob volley.
3. Player A hits a controlled overhead to player B's feet.
4. Player B hits a volley.
5. Player A hits a lob volley.
6. Player B hits a overhead.
7. Player A hits a volley, and so on.

5.2.6 I've included Pepper, even though it takes a considerable degree of skill and a lot of nerve to play, because I love it. This drill is so fast and focused that your mind cannot keep up. Your body takes over and before you know it extraordinary shots are commonplace.

5.3 Full-Court Drills

The full-court drills focus on building consistency and accuracy by hitting crosscourt and down the line. The drills in this section specifically relate to Chapter 3, One Up and One Back.

Most of these practices use two live balls with four players on the court, so you get to hit many more balls than you would playing doubles points. For the practices with two live balls, use either the left or the right side of the court so that you're hitting from a doubles perspective. You may want to place court markers from the center line to the center mark, as shown in diagram 5.3.1. This line becomes one of the side boundaries for your shots.

When hitting crosscourt from the baseline, if you're drawn in to the service line on a short ball, stay in and play the rest of the rally or point from your Workhorse home.

To work on your poaching skills, hitting fed balls is helpful. Use a ball machine or have your practice partner feed you balls from a basket. Play Crosscourt Games to practice poaching in a live ball setting.

Once you get used to hitting with two live balls on one court, you'll find you can focus on your own rally even when hitting crosscourt. As you focus, be mindful that you're sharing the court. Hit with control and don't get in the way of the other player hitting on your end.

Full-Court Drills | Crosscourt groundstrokes

Builds your groundstroke consistency, movement and placement skills.

- For two or four players. If four on court, two live balls will be used at once.
- 10 to 15 minutes.

Full-court crosscourt practice is essential for improving your groundstrokes and should be included in every practice. There are countless ways to modify this drill to keep it interesting.

Directions

Start from the correct baseline home as shown in the diagram. You may want to place some court markers to divide the court in two. As you rally, be sure to turn your body so you're facing both the ball and your hitting partner.

1. Rally crosscourt groundstrokes for five to seven minutes or play the first to seven points.
   - Keep coming back to your home and hit both forehands and backhands.
   - Don't hit balls before they bounce if you're hitting from the correct baseline home. Even though doing so keeps the rally going and may feel good, it trains the inappropriate action of hitting a ball that would land out.
2. Change sides and repeat.

5.3.1 When hitting crosscourt, vary the height, speed, direction, depth and spin of your shots. Always imagine that there's a net player in front of you looking to poach your crosscourt shot. Keep your shots out of his range.

Full-Court Drills | Crosscourt-groundstroke variations

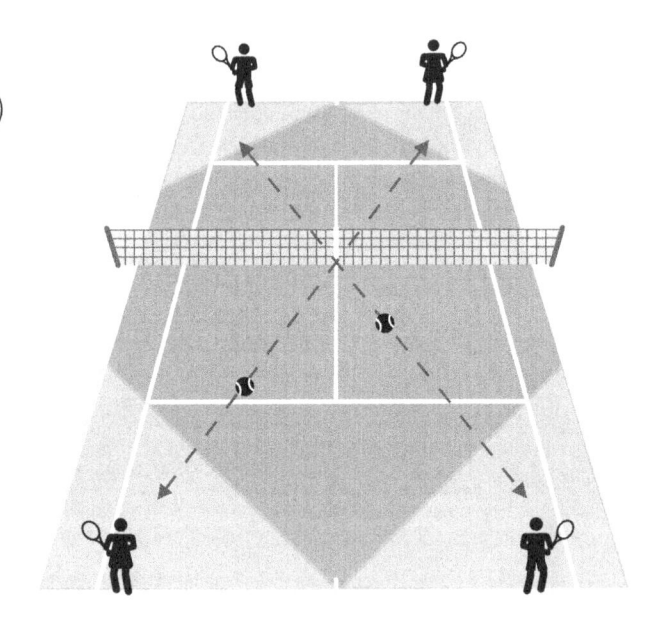

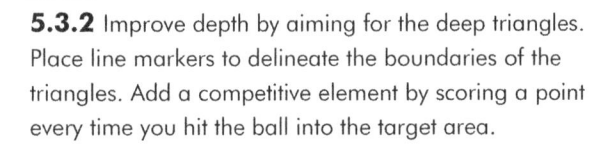

5.3.2 Improve depth by aiming for the deep triangles. Place line markers to delineate the boundaries of the triangles. Add a competitive element by scoring a point every time you hit the ball into the target area.

5.3.3 Improve accuracy by making the court area you're aiming for smaller. Add a competitive element by playing out points in the reduced area.

Full-Court Drills | Hitting straight

Improves your reactions at net and accuracy from the baseline.

- For two or four players. If four on court, two live balls will be used at once.
- 12 to 16 minutes.

"Hitting straight" is different than what occurs in the warm-up before a doubles match because the baseline player is intentionally hitting challenging shots, including down-the-alley shots and power shots directly at the net player.

Directions

Start from the correct baseline and net player homes.

1. Rally down the line for three to four minutes.
    - The baseline player hits some balls hard at the net player and others down the alley.
    - The net player plays reflex volleys back.
2. Change positions (baseline and net) and rally for three to four minutes.
3. Change sides (ad and deuce) and repeat Steps 1 and 2.

Variations: The baseline player can include short lobs, where the net player can hit the overhead from within the service box, or alternate between a short lob and a drive. Deep lobs aren't allowed in this drill because, when playing a doubles point, the deep lobs are covered by the net player's partner (the Workhorse).

5.3.4 Notice that the net players are both playing from their Terminator home, as they're directly across from the ball. When you're the baseline player, make an effort to run to get all balls on the first bounce. If you get drawn in to the net, stay and play racquet-to-racquet volleys to the end of the point.

Full-Court Drills | Lob and neutralizing the lob

Practices your lob and develops your ability to return a lob with a groundstroke drive.

- For two or four players. If four on court, two live balls will be used at once.
- 10 to 12 minutes.

The lob is an essential doubles shot that many players don't take the time to practice. This drill is especially useful in the beginning stages of learning how to lob.

"Neutralizing the lob" is hitting a lob back with a groundstroke drive as opposed to lobbing it back. This skill is important when playing opponents who regularly lob from the baseline or when you're covering a lob from the baseline that's traveled over your partner at net.

Directions

All players start from their baseline homes.
1. Two players lob back and forth from baseline for two to four minutes, aiming for a depth target about halfway between the service line and baseline.
2. One player continues to lob. The second player neutralizes the lob, sending it back as a groundstroke drive. Continue for four minutes.
3. Change the roles of lobber and neutralizer. Continue for four minutes.

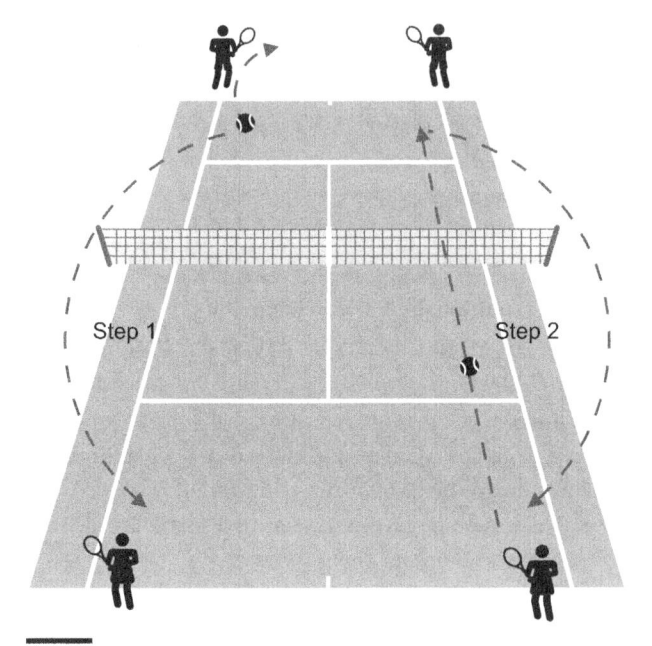

Variation: Play in a crosscourt direction.

5.3.5 When receiving a lob, take your racquet back early and keep your feet moving until just before you hit the ball. Hit through the ball at shoulder height if necessary. Take the opportunity to practice sending and receiving lobs from both your forehand and backhand side.

Full-Court Drills | Crosscourt games

Builds familiarity with playing in the one-up and one-back formation.

- For four players with one live ball.
- 20 minutes.

As a coach, I regularly use this game to isolate a particular skill needed within a one-up and one-back point. When you don't take the time to serve and return, you get many more repetitions of the skill on which you're working.

Directions

Set up as if you're in the middle of a point, playing one up and one back. The baseline players are diagonal to each other on the deuce side and net players diagonal to each other on the ad side.

1. One of the baseline players starts the rally with a forehand groundstroke, aiming the first ball a couple of feet past the service line. The baseline players continue the rally crosscourt while the net players attempt to poach any ball that comes in range. Continue for five minutes, or keep score, playing games to five or seven points.
2. After five minutes or one game, the baseline players change positions with the net players.

Repeat Steps 1 and 2 with the baseline players starting on the ad side and net players on the deuce side.

5.3.6 Many of the skills from Chapter 3, One Up and One Back (for example, baseline player skills, net player poaching skills, defense in offense, covering the lob) can be practiced using this basic set-up. Depending on which skill you're working on, lobs or down-the-alley shots may be allowed or encouraged.

Full-Court Drills | Dingles (singles + doubles)

Improves groundstroke consistency and the ability to expand your focus.

- For four players. Each point begins with two live balls and progresses to one live ball.
- 10 to 15 minutes.

I learned this game from Collin Crawford at a USPTA Western N.Y. coaches' clinic. My students loved it from the get-go.

Directions

All four players begin at their playing-straight baseline homes.

1. Play begins with the two separate singles rallies, playing between the doubles sideline and an imaginary line extending from the center line to the the center mark.
2. When the first of the two balls goes dead (a player misses or hits outside of his boundary), a player calls "dingles."
3. Play continues as a regular doubles point, now with all four players, using the ball that's still in play. A point is scored by the team who wins this point. Play games to five.
4. Change sides, moving from ad to deuce and vice versa.

Variation: Play the two singles rallies in a crosscourt direction. Use the doubles sideline.

5.3.7 This game makes a fun warm-up and works with all levels of players. It's good for breaking the ice if players don't know each other.

5.4 In the Zone Drills

This section includes two step-by-step series (progressions) that focus on Workhorse skills: Workhorse Progression and First-Volley Deep. It also includes a Dogfight and a Both-Back drill.

Both the intention and technique of the Workhorse's volleys are different from the Terminator's.

- As Workhorse, your intention is almost always to hit the ball deep crosscourt in order to set up your Terminator partner.
- As your ability to direct your volleys improves, work on refining your targets, hitting the inside ball closer to the middle and the outside ball more angled (see diagram 4.3.6).
- You must be very centered and alert to respond to all the possible shots for which you're responsible.
- Your volley technique often requires some follow-through or lift to get the ball deep.
- On a low ball, it helps to have a wide base, bend your knees and get your center of gravity low. Move forward to try and hit the ball before it bounces.
- Even when you're making an effort to move forward on low balls, you'll end up hitting half-volleys some of the time.

© CHUCK WILLS

Learning to play the Workhorse is one of the biggest challenges of staggered offense. Regular practice outside of match play is essential to get comfortable, consistent and effective in playing this position.

In the Zone Drills | Workhorse progression (stages one and two)

Improves your volley skills and develops your ability to play the Workhorse position.

- For two or four players. If four on court, two live balls will be used at once.
- 50 minutes.

This co-operative drill gradually moves you back to the Workhorse position. The entire progression will take nearly an hour, with three-minute increments, both partners hitting volleys and groundstrokes and covering ad and deuce sides. For a shorter practice, skip some stages or use shorter increments. Less advanced players may need many practice sessions before becoming proficient at the final stage.

Directions

Follow Steps 1 through 3 for each of the four stages.

Stage 1: Crosscourt mini-tennis with one at net.

Step 1. One (or two players if four on court) player plays at net, halfway between net and service line. The other plays from the just behind the service line. Rally crosscourt for three minutes, with the net player hitting volleys (shown on diagram 5.2.3).

Step 2. Change positions. Rally crosscourt for three minutes.

Step 3. Change sides (deuce to ad) and repeat Steps 1 and 2.

5.4.1 Stage 2: Crosscourt volley to three-quarter court groundstroke. One player hits volleys from halfway between the net and service line. The other hits groundstrokes from the three-quarter court. This position challenges both players to hit the ball farther and to anticipate the ball coming from a greater distance.

In the Zone Drills | Workhorse progression (stages three and four)

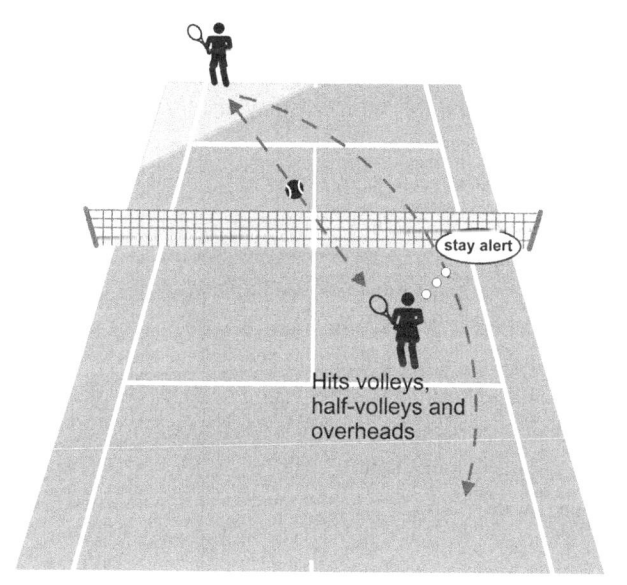

5.4.2 Stage 3: Workhorse to three-quarter court groundstroke. One player hits volleys from the Workhorse home in front of the service line. The other hits groundstrokes from the three-quarter court. This position continues to challenge players to hit the ball farther. Note that the three-quarter court is used as a progressive tool. It's not intended that players should play full-court tennis from the three-quarter court position.

5.4.3 Final stage: Workhorse to baseline. Once volleys are well developed and players can rally consistently from the Workhorse home to the baseline, the other three stages don't need to be practiced. The crosscourt lob and overhead are included in the final stage.

In the Zone Drills | First-volley deep (stage one)

Provides a method for improving your approach shots and first volleys.

- Most comfortable with two players, though can be practiced with four players and two live balls.
- 40 minutes.

My partner Anne Marie Vick and I developed this drill after I watched the finals of the 2008 Senior Women's World Championships. I observed that these players never missed a first volley and consistently returned deep.

First-Volley Deep follows on nicely from the final stage of the Workhorse Progression drill. It provides an ideal opportunity to practice the refined Workhorse volley targets (see diagram 4.3.6).

Directions

There are three stages, each building on the next. In each stage the point is played out crosscourt and the first volley target is deep crosscourt. The baseline player can use any crosscourt shot, including lobs.

The net player and baseline player change roles after three minutes or after a certain number of points are played. The diagrams show play on the ad side only. Both sides should be practiced.

Variation: Keep score, only counting the point after Player B hits a successful shot, thereby giving Player A an attempt to hit a first volley on every point.

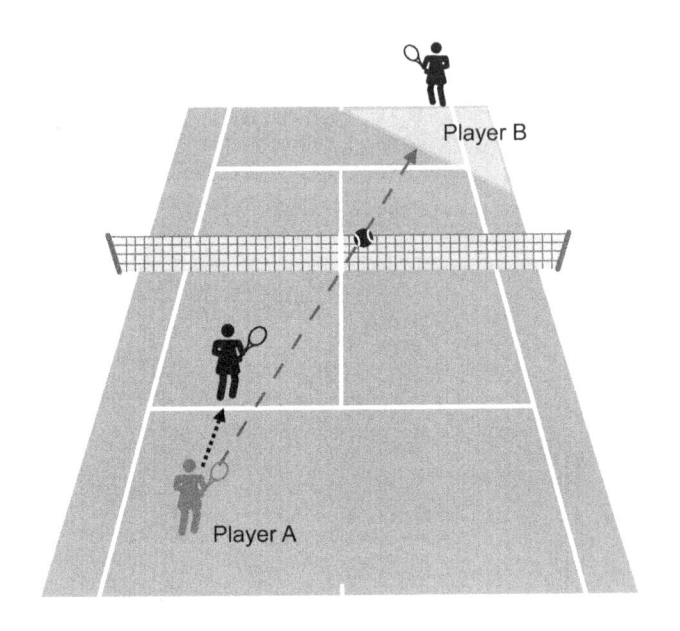

5.4.4 Stage 1: Approach-shot movement pattern. Using an underhand feed, Player A hits an easy ball to the opposite baseline player (simulating the approach shot) and moves to the Workhorse home in the offense zone. Player B returns crosscourt and Player A aims the first volley deep. The point is played out in a crosscourt direction.

In the Zone Drills | First-volley deep (stages two and three)

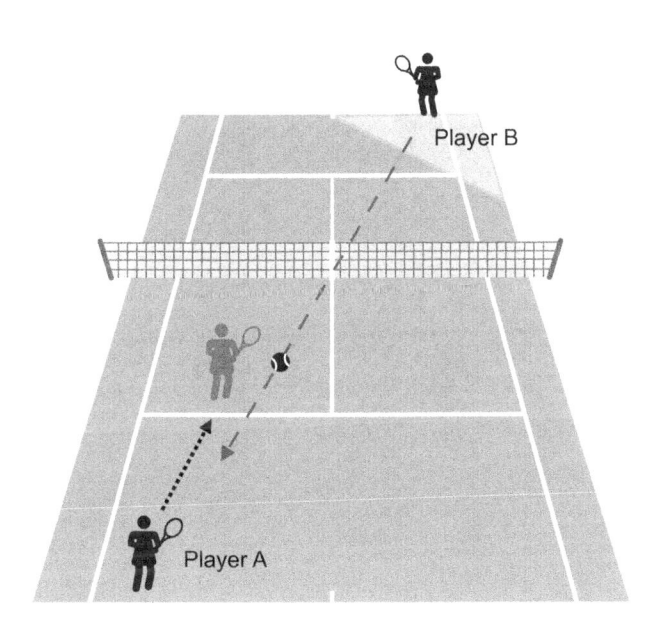

5.4.5 Stage 2: Crosscourt approach from a short ball. Player B feeds a short ball to player A, aiming it around the service line. Player A hits a crosscourt approach shot, moves to the Workhorse home, split steps and gets ready to hit the first volley. The point is played out in a crosscourt direction.

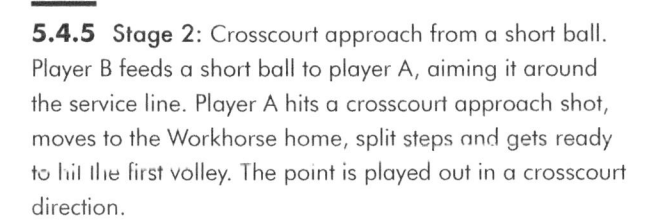

5.4.6 Stage 3: Return and approach. Player B serves second serves. Player A approaches on the return and the point is played out in a crosscourt direction.

Advanced variation: Player B is allowed to hit lobs straight ahead over an imaginary Terminator. Player A runs to the other side to cover the lob and hits down the line. The point continues in a straight direction (see diagram 5.3.4).

In the Zone Drills | Dogfight

Practices the Dogfight (all-four-up formation) and quickens your reactions when playing at net.

- For four players with one live ball.
- 10 minutes.

This is a favorite game for coaches to play during class and students never seem to tire of it. It's also an easy game to play with your practice partners as it doesn't necessarily need a coach to feed the first ball.

Directions

Play begins with all four players behind the service line.

1. Player A feeds a ball to the player directly across. Obvious bad feeds are replayed. Once the feed has crossed the net, all four players may begin moving in. Play out the point. All shots are allowed.
2. Play games to five points, rotating all players one position clockwise after each game.

For hints on how to win this game, see diagram 4.5.2.

Variations: Play cooperatively, counting how many balls can be hit in a row, or use a pattern, with one team hitting crosscourt and the other down the line.

5.4.7 This drill is a lot of fun for players of all levels. Because it moves so fast, you're likely to experience the bliss of playing without thought.

In the Zone Drills | Both up against both back

A versatile game that improves your defense and offense skills.

- For four players with one live ball.
- 15 to 20 minutes.

The attacking players must pay close attention to the Workhorse and Terminator roles in this drill. They change depending on which baseline player is hitting the ball.

Directions

Play begins with two players at the baseline and two players staggered at net. Two balls must cross the net before the point is counted.
- The first ball is fed with a forehand groundstroke by a baseline player to the net player directly across.
- The second ball is a volley that must land in the singles court and past the service line.

Once the point is in play, the defending team can use any of the defensive tools: lobs, drives or the short-angle crosscourt (see section 4.8 for both-back tactics).

The attacking team has no restrictions after the first ball, although the recommended tactic is to hit all balls straight ahead to take away the baseline player's angles (see diagrams 4.7.1 to 4.7.2b). Play games to five or seven points, changing roles after each game.

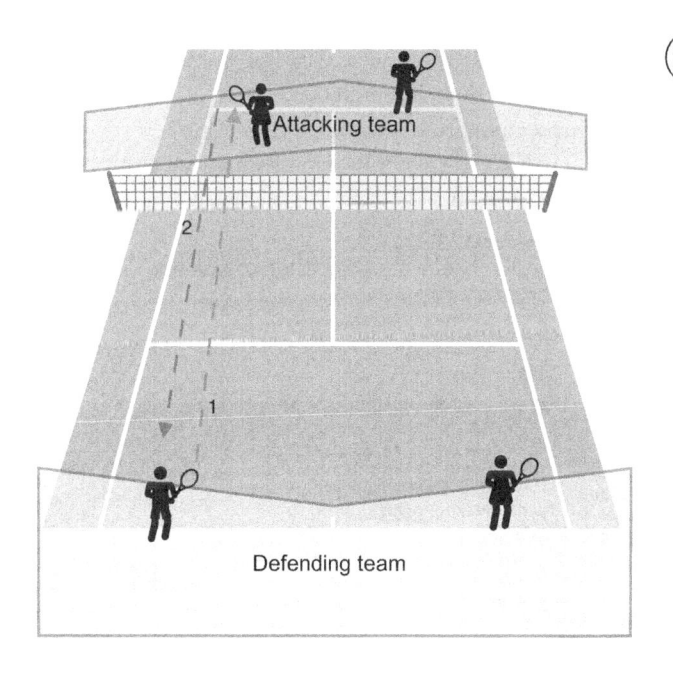

5.4.8 There's a lot more time than you might think when playing from the defense zone. Don't be in a rush to move in. Let every ball bounce and see how long you can make each point last.

5.5 Serve and Return Drills

It makes good sense to practice both serve and return, as many points are won or lost in these first two shots. Practicing these shots will give you immediate improvement in your match play.

This section provides ideas for serve and return practice that will keep things interesting and help you develop new skills. These drills specifically relate to Chapter 2, Starting the Point.

I suggest you allocate some time to practice both serve and return in every practice session.

Serve and Return Drills | Serve practice

Provides an opportunity to develop your serve in a non-pressure situation.

- For one or two players.
- 15 to 30 minutes.

Practicing your serve is akin to a golf player going to the driving range. It's surprising that most tennis players don't take advantage of the ease of practicing the serve.

- Serve practice allows you to feel the flow of your serving motion without the usual pressure to get the ball in. If you're making technical changes, definitely practice your serve outside of point play.
- Hopefully you're getting in most of your first serves during your matches. Use some of your practice time to keep your second serve tuned up.

Directions

Once you can get your serve in the box, always have a target in mind before you serve. Focus on different aspects to make your practice time more productive.

- If making technical changes, practice one swing without the ball in between each serve.
- Alternate between first and second serves, deuce and ad sides.
- Practice the serve and volley movement pattern.
- Count how many serves you can make out of 10.
- Develop and practice your serve ritual.

Serving can be practiced on your own. All you need is a hopper of balls.

Serve and Return Drills | Serve depth and direction

Dramatically improves the effectiveness of your serve.

- For one or two players.
- 15 to 30 minutes.

Directions

Create depth and direction target areas with rows of line markers.

1. For depth, place a line halfway between the net and service line. As you improve, place the line farther back.
   - If most balls are landing short in the service box, aim past the service line.
   - If many balls are landing long, adjust your technique. Add more spin, toss and reach up higher, or emphasize the pronation action of your forearm.
2. For direction, place two rows of markers to make three vertical areas for the T, body serve (B), and angled serve (A). Practice all three directions.
   - To hit a particular direction, first visualize where you want to serve.
   - Place your serve by making adjustments to the racquet angle and varying your spin.
   - If you hit with slice, aim your serve farther to the right (for right-handers) or left (for left-handers).

5.5.1 To help you focus and track your improvement, add a measurable goal, such as making at least seven out of 10 balls into a designated area. As your placement improves, practice both depth and direction simultaneously. Remember to practice placement on both first and second serves.

Serve and Return Drills | How to serve and volley

Provides a method for learning to serve and volley.

- Most comfortable with two players, though can be practiced with four players and two live balls.
- 15 to 20 minutes.

The serve and volley is a skill that's definitely worth having in your doubles toolbox. Start by practicing on your own. Once you know the basics, practice with a Receiver so you can time your split step and hit a first volley.

Directions

1. After your serve motion is complete, continue to run forward about three to four steps.
2. Slow down when the ball bounces on the other side and split step as the Receiver strikes the ball.
- Most players will only make it somewhere into the transition zone. That's OK. Make your split step there.
- A serve hit deep and with spin will give you more time to get in than a power serve.
3. Move toward the ball as it comes off the Receiver's racquet. Hit your volley before the bounce if you can, otherwise use a half-volley.
4. Recover to the Workhorse home inside the service line.

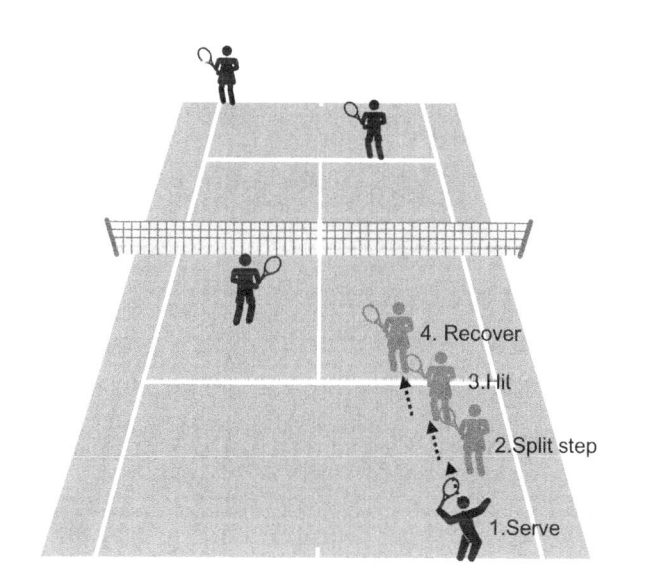

5.5.2 After your serve, make it as far into the court as you can, but be sure to pause and split step before the Receiver hits the ball. The first volley is usually hit from within the transition zone, after which you recover to the Workhorse home.

Serve and Return Drills | Learn to serve and volley

5.5.3 Stage 1: Serve and volley movement pattern. Practice the forward movement making your serve motion without a ball (not shown).
Stage 2: Serve and volley without a Receiver. Practice the forward movement after your serve. Slow down as the ball bounces, split step, then take another couple of steps and hit an imaginary first volley.

5.5.4 Stage 3: Serve and volley practice with a Receiver. Play out the point crosscourt. In the beginning, the Receiver hits easy crosscourt returns. Later on, a wide variety of crosscourt returns, including lobs, can be hit to challenge the Server's first volley skills.

Serve and Return Drills | Crosscourt return practice

Builds confidence and consistency in your crosscourt return.

- For two or four players. If four on court, two live balls will be used.
- Six to 15 minutes.

A few missed returns can make a difference between winning and losing a match. It makes sense to practice this important shot. If you specialize on the ad or deuce side, use your time wisely and only practice returns on your chosen side. Remember to practice both first and second serve returns.

Directions

In this practice, focus on your return without playing out the point. As the Receiver, you can ask the Server to aim for a particular spot or to mix things up.

Aim the majority of your returns to the deep-crosscourt triangle. The short-crosscourt triangle is a good choice on a serve that lands short and near the sideline.

The Server's role is to support the player returning. Just serve. Don't hit the return back. You may want to serve from the three-quarter court to achieve more power or greater consistency. Serve from a position closer to the doubles sideline to hit an angled serve.

Change the role of Server and Receiver every three to five minutes.

5.5.5 When practicing returns, visualize before the Server hits the ball where you plan to return the serve. Remember to keep in mind where the opposing net player would be and hit your crosscourt return to avoid this player.

Serve and Return Drills | Specialty shot return practice

Builds experience, confidence and consistency in your down-the-line speciality returns.

- For two or three players. Perfect for three players. If only two players, place a cone or chair in the position of Server's Partner.
- 12 to 18 minutes.

A speciality shot is a down-the-line return that's used to avoid an active poacher. Study the material on speciality shots (diagrams 2.5.8 and 2.5.9) before doing this practice.

Don't try to develop every shot. Choose one shot on the forehand and one on the backhand to develop and practice. If you specialize on a particular side, develop your shots on your chosen side.

Directions

Each player gets four to six minutes to practice their specialty returns. The Server and Server's Partner are both in support roles.

The Server needs to be consistent. Serve from inside the baseline at three-quarter court if needed. Don't hit or run after the returns.

Server's Partner stands in the usual starting location, pretending not to know the Receiver is hitting down the line. Server's Partner should hit the Receiver's shot if it's in his range. Don't play out the point after that.

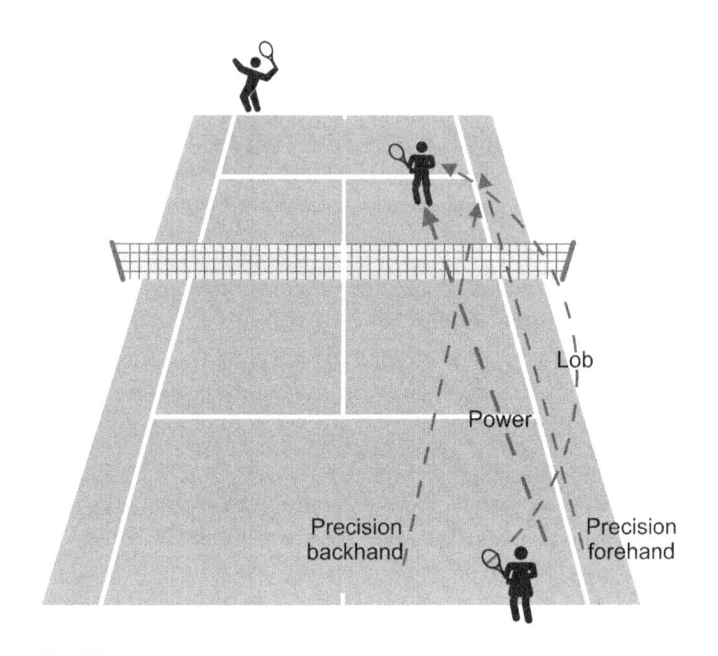

5.5.6 In match play, the majority of returns should be hit crosscourt. However, having the confidence to hit down the line at the right moment is a valuable skill. It's a good investment to use some of your practice time to develop your specialty shots.

5.6 Games for Two or Three

Sometimes you want to practice doubles points but don't have a foursome, or perhaps you have planned a match and one player cancels at the last minute.

This section details how you can play points and games that resemble doubles with only two or three players.

If you're practicing with two or three players, you can use these games for point play near the end of your practice session. This helps to integrate the skills you have worked on.

Dedicated doubles players use every opportunity to practice doubles-related shots and skills.

Games for Two or Three | Ghost doubles

Improves consistency on your serve, return, crosscourt groundstrokes and Workhorse volleys.

- For two to four players. If four on court, two crosscourt points can be played simultaneously.
- 10 to 30 minutes.

Ghost doubles is an ideal way to hit a lot of balls and play practice points. It's good for all levels of players including beginners.

Directions

Place line markers between the center line and center mark to create two separate court areas, as shown.

Play out crosscourt points, including a serve and return. The deep-crosscourt triangles are your primary targets. You can play from the baseline or approach the net. Because you're diagonal to the ball, remember to play the Workhorse role if you approach the net. As the baseline player, pay attention and hit a crosscourt lob if your opponent moves in too close to the net.

To keep score, play four points with the same Server on one side. If the score is two all after four points, play a tiebreak point. Change servers and play four points. Change sides (deuce to ad) and repeat.

With only two players on the court, you may enjoy using regular game scoring, alternating sides after each point.

5.6.1 Ghost doubles gets its name from the fact that your doubles partner in this game is imaginary.

Games for Two or Three | Australian ghost doubles

5.6.2 Ad-court Australian for two players. Serve from the ad side and move to cover the deuce. Receiver returns straight ahead, into the deuce half of the court. Play the point out in a straight direction. Note: The two faint players on the non-playing side represent the ghost players.

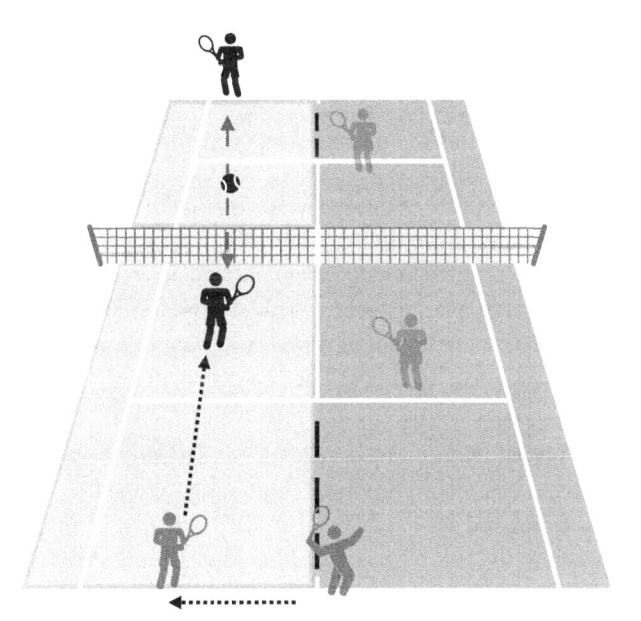

5.6.3 Deuce-court Australian for two players. Serve from the deuce side and move to cover the ad. Either player can approach net, moving to the Terminator home. Lobs are not allowed as they belong to the (imaginary) Workhorse. Note: The two faint players on the non-playing side represent the ghost players.

Games for Two or Three | Puerto Rican doubles

Provides a way to play with three people that's tactically similar to doubles.

- For three players.
- 20 to 60 minutes.

I created and named this game on vacation in Puerto Rico. It differs from the traditional three-person "doubles" game, often called Canadian doubles. Canadian doubles, though fun to play, makes no tactical sense from either a doubles or singles point of view. If you want to practice your doubles skills, choose Puerto Rican doubles.

Directions

This is a two-on-one doubles game. The single player is the Server. Play out points, alternating serving from the deuce and ad sides. The team with two players must play into the side of the court (including the alleys) from where the Server started the point. This means the Receiver must hit the return crosscourt.

The single player (Server) can hit into the entire doubles court. Notice that the Server serves from the doubles serving position, since he's only covering one side of the court.

There are no limitations on the type of shot allowed. The only restriction is the deuce- or ad-court boundary. Change Server and the two-on-one combination after every game. Score one point for each game won.

5.6.4 This diagram shows the playing area for the deuce side point. As in regular doubles, the Server alternates sides, covering the ad side of the court on the second point. Note that Receiver's Partner doesn't have to start on the service line as there's no Server's Partner to present any danger.

Games for Two or Three | Puerto Rican variations

5.6.5 When playing Puerto Rican doubles, feel free to modify who serves and how you rotate. When a player on the two-player team serves, the Receiver has the opportunity to practice both crosscourt and down-the-line returns.

5.6.6 You can practice Australian formation and playing straight with this three-player set up. The Server moves to the other side after serving and the Receiver must return down the line. If the sole player moves into net, lobs are not allowed (for explanation, see diagram 5.6.3)

5.7 Warm-ups

When competing, doing an on-court warm-up before your match helps to prepare your body and settle your nerves. It's especially important to do if you consider yourself to be a "slow starter."

When you have already warmed up before the match, you have more freedom to pay attention to your opponents' strengths and weaknesses during the 10 minutes allowed before you start game play.

If you can't fit in an on-court warm-up before your match, find a way to loosen up your body by biking on a stationary bike, jumping rope, or jogging. Yoga is also a good choice, as it helps focus and calm your mind while warming and stretching your muscles.

If all else fails and you haven't had a chance to warm-up, spend a few quiet moments before your match visualizing yourself playing your best doubles tennis. Imagine yourself playing the first couple of games, moving and hitting with confidence and ease.

Warming up with your partner, either on or off the court, gives you extra time to tune in with each other before your match begins.

Warm-ups | Pre-match routine

Prepares your body and mind for match play.

- For two or four players.
- 30 to 45 minutes.

Most players find it helpful to warm up on a court prior to a match. Warm up close to the time of your match if possible. If that's not available, it's still beneficial to do a warm-up at any time on the day of your match.

- A pre-match warm-up gets your strokes in a groove before you head out for your match.
- It gives you a chance to hit all of your strokes crosscourt: groundstrokes, volleys and overheads.
- It provides an opportunity to hit some service returns.
- It helps you relax.
- When playing outside, it gets you used to the day's elements. Change ends often, especially if it's windy. Serve, return and hit overheads from both ends.

If you have four on the court, two live balls will be used and you'll need to co-operate with the other pair when to change from a down-the-line to crosscourt direction and from the deuce to ad side.

If you must warm up with three players, follow the pattern used in Puerto Rican Doubles, so that doubles shots are being hit. That is, the single player plays from either the deuce or ad side, not the middle. I recommend this because, although hitting with the single player in the middle of the court will warm up your body and strokes, it won't give you the benefit of hitting shots with the proper doubles angles. Change places often so that players get equal time in each location.

The Routine

1. Mini-tennis.
2. Racquet-to-racquet volleys straight.
3. Full-court straight groundstrokes.
4. One at net, one at baseline. Include a few lobs and overheads.
5. Full-court crosscourt groundstrokes.
6. One at net in the Workhorse position, one at baseline. Include lobs and overheads. Change so that the net player becomes the baseline player and vice versa.

Repeat Steps 5 and 6 on the other side of the court.

7. Serve and return. Return only from your side. Serve from both sides.
8. Play ghost doubles. If four players, you may want to play out some regular points.

Keep your warm-up focused and moving along.

- Steps 1–4: one-third of your time.
- Steps 5–6: one-third of your time.
- Steps 7–8: one-third of your time.

Warm-ups | Ten minute half-court warm-up

Loosens and warms up your body. Encourages focus, control, cooperation and consistency.

- For two or four players. If four on court, two live balls will be used at once.
- 10 minutes. Use a timer if you have one as a minute goes by faster than you might think.

I learned this warm-up during a Professional Tennis Registry (PTR) Adult Development Certification course. I've taken the liberty to add "half-court" into the name to distinguish it from the standard sequence used before a social or competitive match (see next page).

- Use it to start a practice session or as a pre-match warm-up if you're short on time.

Directions

Play each of the five stages for two minutes. In each stage, Player A and B switch roles after one minute.

1. Player A (in the near court) hits groundstrokes to Player B's forehand volley.
2. Player A hits groundstrokes to Player B's backhand volley.
3. Player A hits groundstrokes, alternating to Player B's forehand and backhand volley.
4. Player A hits a short lob to Player B. Player B hits a soft overhead toward Player A's feet.
5. Combination: Player A hits to Player B's forehand volley, then backhand volley, then hits a short lob.

5.7.1 Although this is called a warm-up, it's also great for improving volley consistency. Use it to build the skills so you can play Pepper (see diagram 5.2.6).

Warm-ups | Standard ten minute warm-up

Allows you to hit all strokes prior to your match while observing your opponent.

- Four players and two live-ball rallies. Except for the serves, you'll be hitting straight on two half-courts.
- 10 minutes. Times in parenthesis are my guidelines.

This is the standard sequence used before a competitive or social match. Warm up with the three balls you'll use in the match. Usually another three good quality balls are also used, making six balls in total on the court.

Be a good sport and give your opponent a proper warm-up. Do your best to keep the ball in play. If you're uncomfortable with any step, address it in one of your practice sessions. In particular, learn to send consistent lobs.

1. Mini-tennis. (optional, one minute)
2. Groundstrokes straight. (three minutes)
3. One at net, one at baseline. Include volleys, lobs and overheads. (one to two minutes)
4. Switch positions, net and baseline. Repeat step 3. (one to two minutes)
5. Serve. (two to three minutes)

Each player takes three to six serves on each side. Don't return the serves. Just catch them and serve them back. With practice, you'll become efficient at warming up serves. Never skip this step, even in social matches. It's important for warming up your shoulder.

START HERE

KEEP IT MOVING / GET WHAT YOU NEED

10 MINUTE WARM-UP

- mini-tennis 1 min. — *"Would you like to move back?"*
- serving practice 2–3 min.
- groundstrokes straight 3 min. — *"Can you give me some backhands?"*
- one at net, one at baseline 1–2 min. — *"Do you want some volleys?"*
- switch net and baseline 1–2 min. — *"Can I have a couple up?"*
- *"Ready for serves?"*

STRATEGY: Pay attention to whether the opponent you're hitting with is right- or left-handed, prefers forehand or backhand, and how comfortable he is at net and with sending lobs. Take note of anything unusual, such as a heavy slice backhand or two-handed forehand. Also notice the depth, speed and usual direction of his serve. Give a brief synopsis to your partner before the match begins.

Practice Skills | Summary

Why Practice?
- Practice will accelerate your rate of improvement. Plan your practice to enhance your strengths and improve your weaknesses.
- Be deliberate with how and where you hit every shot as you practice. If you're losing focus, keep score or move to another drill.
- In every practice session include some racquet-to-racquet volleys, crosscourt groundstrokes, and serve and return practice. Conclude with at least a few minutes of point play.

Half-Court Drills
- The half-court drills are excellent for developing your reflexes, and the consistency and accuracy of your volleys.
- The crosscourt Mini-Tennis practice is an efficient and effective way to practice the different volley angles you need as a net player.

Full-Court Drills
- The full-court drills are designed to help you practice the skills you need to execute the tactics described in Chapter 3, One Up and One Back.
- When practicing crosscourt and straight groundstrokes, use the correct baseline homes and always imagine where the opposing net player would be if you were playing a doubles point.
- To improve your poaching skills, play Crosscourt Games or have your partner or a ball machine feed you balls.

In the Zone Drills
- Use the Workhorse Progression drill to improve your crosscourt volleys and develop the ability to be consistent and effective playing the Workhorse.
- Use the First-Volley Deep drill to practice approach shots and refine your first volley.

Serve and Return Drills
- Practicing your serve and return will result in immediate improvement in your match play.
- If you're working on changing anything technical in your serve, practice your serve regularly outside of match play until the change becomes integrated.

Games for Two or Three
- Ghost Doubles allows you to play doubles points with only two players.
- Puerto Rican Doubles is a game played with three players that closely resembles the positioning and shot angles of four-person doubles.

Warm-Ups
- Use the standard 10 Minute Warm-Up as an opportunity to assess your opponents' strengths and weaknesses before your match begins.

CONCLUSION

I hope that *On the Ball* is already enriching your doubles game.

Use *On the Ball* to become the best partner you can be. If you have the good fortune to have a regular partner, take the opportunity to develop together. When playing with other partners, be patient with those who don't know the correct positioning. Consider setting up a practice group amongst your team or group of friends so that the number of players who know the system grows. To connect with other like-minded players worldwide, join the the Facebook community: *On the Ball – Adventures in Doubles Tennis*.

More than anything, *On the Ball* teaches how to focus attention during a point. The shot cycle provides the blueprint for how to expand awareness in the few seconds when the ball is actually in play. As you train and embody all the elements of the shot cycle, it'll feel like you have more time.

Your opponent's impact and your impact are the two key moments in this model. At your impact, have a single point of focus as you keep your eyes on the ball. For an instant, nothing exists beyond your racquet, mind, body and ball. Then immediately focus on recovery to your correct home to be in the best position to hit the next ball. Avoid the trap of admiring or judging the shot you've just hit.

At your opponent's impact, be centered, all the way from the balls of your feet as you split step, to your mind, clear and ready to respond. Also be aware of the opponent who's hitting the ball, her positioning, balance, racquet and even her facial expression. It turns out that the ability to be centered in yourself, while being aware of what's going on around you, is an advanced skill that's useful in many situations in daily life.

The opportunity to learn and play the complex and challenging game of tennis is a great gift. I hope this book helps you enjoy your tennis journey to the fullest, brings you to a new level of competence in your doubles game, and opens you to the joy of working together seamlessly with your partner.

Gyata Stormon

I'd love to hear how you're doing and what questions you have. You can reach me at ontheballbook@gmail.com. Subscribe to my mailing list at: www.ontheballbook/subscribe.

APPENDIX: GUIDE FOR BEGINNERS

As a beginner, you can practice and play games from the get-go. Even if you can't keep a rally going at the full court, you can play with softer balls in a half or three-quarter court.

Use this book to teach you to play tactically correct doubles. Some of the things you'll learn include: where to stand on the court, which ball belongs to you, and where to hit the ball. The following list will direct you to the skills you need to develop first.

CHAPTER 1: ORIENTATION

Start by reading all of this chapter. Pay particular attention to the following pages:

1.2 Court Geography (p. 21)
- The homes
- The one-up and one-back formation
- Doubles zones
- Guide to diagrams
- Lines and dimensions

CHAPTER 2: STARTING THE POINT

Focus on the following pages. Skip the sections and pages not listed until you're confident with all of the skills in the pages listed below.

2.1 The Four Starting Positions (p. 30)
- Starting locations vary

2.3 The Server (p. 35)
- The serve ritual
- Placing the serve
- First and second serves

2.4 Server's Partner (p. 43)
- Support the server in between points
- Starting location
- Dealing with powerful returns

2.5 The Receiver (p. 51)
- Be a good sport
- Starting location
- Starting location varies
- Hit most returns crosscourt
- Other crosscourt returns (low crosscourt lob only)
- The short serve

2.6 Receiver's Partner (p. 63)
- Hot-seat procedure
- Defensive starting locations

CHAPTER 3: ONE UP AND ONE BACK

3.1 One-up and one-back formation (p. 86)
- Target areas

3.2 The Net Player (p. 88)
- Play from the correct home
- How to poach
- To poach or not to poach
- Get out of trouble
- Gaze points
- Develop a "good eye"

3.3 The Baseline Player (p. 103)
- Play from the correct home
- Win from the baseline
- Change the direction
- Hit down the alley
- Set up the net player
- Baseline player moves to the net
- Trouble shooting

3.4 The Lob (p. 114)
- Mine or yours?
- Covering with a switch
- Covering with a stay

3.5 Playing Straight (p. 121)
- Net player's home
- Baseline player's home

© GYATA STORMON

As soon as you can get your serve in the box, at least some of the time, start playing doubles games. Look for a group of players with a similar ability, or include one or two experienced players who are willing to help you along.

CHAPTER 4: IN THE ZONE

I suggest you wait to work on this chapter until you're confident with the entire One-Up and One-Back chapter. As soon as you feel ready, you can use the Workhorse Progression exercises to develop the specific volley skills you'll need when you get to this chapter (diagrams 5.4.1 to 5.4.3).

CHAPTER 5: PRACTICE SKILLS

The key to learning to play tennis is to practice regularly with one or more practice partners. Even if you're a complete beginner, you can find ways to practice that are fun and will help you improve. Design your practice session from the drills listed below.

5.1 Why Practice? (p. 184)
- Ball machine or live ball
- Tips for live-ball practice
- Practice safely

5.2 Half-Court Drills (p. 188)
- Mini-tennis
- Crosscourt mini-tennis
- Racquet-to-racquet volleys

5.3 Full-Court Drills (p. 194)
- Crosscourt groundstrokes
- Hitting straight
- Lob and neutralizing the lob
- Crosscourt games
- Dingles
- Workhorse progression (stages one and two)

5.5 Serve and Return Drills (p. 208)
- Serve practice
- Serve depth and direction
- Crosscourt return practice

5.6 Games for Two or Three (p. 215)
- Ghost doubles
- Puerto Rican doubles
- Pre-match return (suitable as a practice routine, exclude step six)
- Standard ten minute warm-up

BIBLIOGRAPHY

Antoun, Rob. 2007. *Women's Tennis Tactics.* Champaign, IL: Human Kinetics

Blaskower, Pat. 2007. *The Art of Doubles*, 2nd edition. Cincinnati, OH: Betterway Books

Cayer, Louis. 2004. *Doubles Tennis Tactics,* Champaign, IL: Human Kinetics

Clarke, Valerie and Gyata Stormon. 2019. *The Play Book.* Email theplaybookdrills@gmail.com for further information.

Elderton, Wayne. 2002. "Are You Learning to Play the Game-Based Way?" www.acecoach.com

Elderton, Wayne. 2018. "The Shot Cycle: Key Building Blocks for Situational Training." www.acecoach.com

Fernandez, Gigi. 2018 "The Gigi Method Doubles Instructional Program." www.doubles.tv

Spang, Peter. 1998. *Zennis.* New York, NY: Penguin Putnam

Sparre, Helle. 2004. *Dynamite Doubles.* Berkeley, CA: Regent Press

Helle Sparre (black shorts) working with Gyata Stormon (center) and Cora Wills in 2011.

GLOSSARY OF TENNIS TERMS

Ad court – The left vertical half of the court.

Approach shot – A shot hit from the transition zone as you move to a new home at the net.

Attack zone – The small area on the tennis court between the offense zone and the net.

Baseline player – The player who plays from her home at the back of the court when playing in the one-up and one-back formation.

Bounce-overhead – A shot where you hit the ball over your head with a serving motion after receiving a lob that bounces high.

Centering moment – A phase of the shot cycle. Your racquet is in ready position, you split step and your mind is clear. It should occur every time your opponent hits the ball.

Continental grip – A neutral position of the hand on the racquet, sometimes known as the "shake-hands grip." This is a good choice for the ready position and is the correct grip for serve and volleys.

Crosscourt – The direction from one end of the court to the other diagonally (for example, from the deuce court at one end to the deuce court at the other end).

Defense zone – The area on the tennis court surrounding the baseline and all the way back to the fence.

Deuce court – The right vertical half of the court.

Dipping shot – A groundstroke hit in such a way that it dips at the opponent's feet.

Down the line – The direction from one end of the court to the other, parallel to the sidelines (for example, from the deuce court at one end to the ad court at the other end).

Drawn in – When your opponent hits a short ball that causes you to run forward from your baseline home to the offense zone.

Drive – A forehand or backhand groundstroke that's hit with pace and travels a low to medium height over the net.

Drop shot – A groundstroke or volley that drops quickly after crossing the net, thereby landing very short in the opponent's court.

Early leave – When the net player moves toward the middle before the opposing baseline player starts his forward swing.

Floater – A mid-height ball hit with little pace.

Groundstroke – A shot, hit from either the right or left side of the body, striking the ball after it bounces.

Half-volley – A shot, hit directly after the bounce, as the ball is rising.

Home – The location on the court where you center yourself and get ready to receive a ball by the time the opposing player hits the ball.

Impact point – The moment the racquet meets the ball.

Inside ball – A ball that doesn't travel across your body as it goes toward your racquet. For a right-handed player, this is a backhand on the deuce side and a forehand on the ad side.

Inside-out crosscourt – A ball hit from the inside of the body sent in a crosscourt direction. For a right-handed player this shot is hit with a backhand from the deuce side and a forehand from the ad side.

Lob – A shot sending the ball high in the air, ideally landing well behind the service line.

Lob volley – A shot hit before the bounce with an open racquet face, sending the ball high in the air.

Net player – The player who plays from her home near the net.

Neutralize a lob – A shot where you receive a lob and hit it back as a drive.

NTRP – A tennis rating program developed by the United States Tennis Association (USTA) that describes the general characteristics of 13 different levels of tennis-playing ability.

Offense zone – The area on the tennis court between the service line and attack zone.

Outside ball – A ball that travels across your body as it goes toward your racquet. For a right-handed player, this is a forehand on the deuce side and backhand on the ad side.

Overhead – A shot where your racquet strikes a high ball above your head with a serving motion.

Playing formation – The arrangement of the players once the point has begun with a serve and return (for example, one up and one back).

Poach – When a player at the net intercepts a ball that was on its way to her partner.

Precision down the line – A specialty shot where the ball is sent down the line with the alley as the intended target.

Quick serve – A serve hit before the Receiver is ready.

Ready position – The position of racquet in centering phase, in front of your body with a neutral grip.

Receiving phase – A stage of the shot cycle that occurs between the time your opponent hits the ball and just before you start your forward swing.

Recovery – Movement to the optimal place on the court (home) after you hit the ball and before the opponent hits the ball. This is the final part of the sending phase.

Reverse stagger – An incorrect both-up formation where the Terminator is diagonal to the ball and the the Workhorse is across from the ball.

Sending phase – A stage of the shot cycle that occurs between the time you start your forward swing, through the impact point, follow-through and recovery.

Shot cycle – A model that describes the way a ball is exchanged between players in three phases: centering, sending and receiving.

Starting location – The place on the court where you choose to begin the point.

Starting position – The role you assume at the beginning of the point: Server, Server's Partner, Receiver or Receiver's Partner.

Specialty shot – A down-the-line shot used to avoid an active net player.

Split step – Gentle bounce on the balls of the feet that balances your entire body and prepares you to move in any direction. It's part of the centering moment and should occur every time the opponent hits the ball.

Skyhook – A type of forehand volley used to reach a deep lob. The ball is hit from behind your body and some follow-through is needed.

Staggered offense – A modern system of positioning when both partners move up to the net (the offense zone). One player (the Terminator) remains closer to the net with the job of putting the ball away to finish the point. The other player (the Workhorse) stays farther back, with the job of setting up the player who is closer to the net and covering the deep lobs.

Strike zone – The most comfortable place to hit the ball, usually in front of the body, waist height on groundstrokes and chest height on volleys.

Swinging volley – A type of volley that uses groundstroke technique. It's often hit at shoulder height and from the transition zone.

Terminator – The net player directly across from the ball that's in the opponent's court. This is the partner closer to the net.

The wall – The traditional method of positioning when both partners are at net, whereby partners line up side by side.

Tie-break – A special game in which the Server changes every two points, played when the game score is six all. It may also be used in lieu of a third set when the score is one set each.

Transition zone – The area on the tennis court between the baseline and service line in which players travel as they move between the offense and defense zones. This is also known as "no-man's land" as there are no homes in this zone.

Volley – A forehand or backhand shot hit before the ball bounces.

Workhorse – The net player diagonal to the ball that's in the opponent's court. This is the partner farther from the net.

CONTACT GYATA STORMON

Keep up to date by subscribing to my email list. Go to *www.ontheballbook.com/subscribe* to sign up.

If you'd like to buy multiple copies of this book for your team, contact me at *ontheballbook@gmail.com*, or email me at the same address with any other comments or questions.

Made in the USA
Coppell, TX
17 December 2019